SECRET POWER

D.L. MOODY

SECRET POWER

D.L. MOODY

Bridge-Logos
Alachua, Florida 32615

Bridge-Logos

Alachua, Florida 32615 USA

Secret Power
by D.L. Moody

Edited by Gene Fedele

Printed in the United States of America.

Library of Congress Catalog Card Number: 2005936838
International Standard Book Number 978-0-88270-114-1

Unless otherwise indicated, Scripture quotations are from the *King James Version* of the Bible.

CONTENTS

INTRODUCTION

"But you shall receive the power of the Holy Spirit coming upon you: and you shall be witnesses unto me both in Jerusalem, and in Judea, and in Samaria, and unto the uttermost part of the earth"(Acts 1:8).

In the eternal and sovereign providence of God, He has chosen to use ordinary people, empowered by the extraordinary Holy Spirit, as the chief means through which He spreads the truths of His Word. Dwight L. Moody was one such man who was filled with power and stood for great truth. "The Spirit of the Lord is upon me, and He has anointed me to preach the gospel." This man, so humble, so sincere, so selfless, so steadfast in his faith in Christ had a special gift of presenting the precious gospel in a way that all could understand.

Moody's life and ministry were constant invitations for sinners to come to Christ. He saw every person, no matter how far from God, as a potential child of the King, and a possible moment from eternity. This was the driving force behind Moody becoming one of the greatest evangelists the world has ever known. "I don't believe that better news fell upon the ears of mortal man, than the news of the gospel." Though he was a man of humble means and little formal education, his passion for the salvation of the lost was a flame that burned ever bright as a light of pure love for God and his fellow man. "It is the greatest pleasure of living to win souls to Christ."

In this book, *Secret Power*, Moody reveals the power behind this "flame," this divine force, as the working of the Holy Spirit in the heart of a man. He believed that this power was received from God when we are completely emptied of self, ready to serve the will of God. He saw it expressed as a balance between zeal and knowledge and that too often Christians would gravitate to one extreme or the other, causing division and fruitlessness in their lives and gospel work, sometimes even bringing reproach upon the name of Christ. We can see a glimpse of this in his chapter on witnessing: "I have no sympathy with those men who try to limit God's salvation to a certain few. I believe that Christ died for all who will come. I have received many letters finding fault with me, and saying I surely don't believe the doctrine of election. I do believe in election; but I have no business to preach that doctrine to the world at large. The world has nothing to do with election; it has only to do with the invitation, 'Whosoever will, let him take the water of life freely.' That is the message for the sinner. I am sent to preach the gospel to all."

His dear friend and fellow preacher, R. A. Torrey, wrote about the seven things in Moody's life that enabled him to be used by God so mightily:

1. **He was a completely surrendered man.** "If you and I are to be used in our sphere as D. L. Moody was in his, we must put all that we have and all that we are in the hands of God, for Him to use as He will, and we on our part do everything God bids us to do."

2. **He was a man of prayer.** "Often we would be gathered until three or four o'clock in the morning,

crying to God, just because Mr. Moody urged us to wait upon God until we received His blessing. Oh, how many men and women whose lives and characters have been transformed by those nights of prayer and who have wrought might things in many lands because of those nights in prayer."

3. **He was a deep and practical student of the Bible.** "Oh, you may talk about power, but if you neglect the one Book that God has given you as the one instrument through which He imparts His power, you will not have it. Ninety-nine Christians in every hundred are merely playing at Bible study; and therefore are mere weaklings, when they might be giants, both in their Christian life and in their service."

4. **He was a humble man.** "D. L. Moody was the humblest man I ever knew. In his heart he constantly underestimated himself and overestimated others. He really believed that God would use other men in a larger measure than he had been used."

5. **He was completely freed from the love of money.** "This is the point where many evangelists make shipwreck. The love of money has done more to discredit evangelistic work in our day than almost any other cause. Millions of dollars passed into Mr. Moody's hands, but they passed through; they did not stick to his fingers."

6. **He was consumed with passion for the salvation of the lost.** "Moody was a man on fire for God. Not only was he 'on the job' himself, but he was always getting others to the work as well. He made a resolution shortly after he, himself, was saved, that he would never allow a day to go by without speaking to at least one person about Christ."

7. He was endued with power from on high.
"... the Holy Ghost came upon him filling his soul with such joy that he had to ask God to withhold His hand, lest he die on the spot from very joy!"

In his 1875 book, *D. L. Moody and His Work*, C. H. Fowler writes, "The Bible is largely made up of biographies; and men see the value of faith and righteousness by seeing the men who believed and obeyed. Abstractions are feeble; but, when a man causes things to come to pass, by studying him we find out some great secret of power. D. L. Moody is one of these men. The study of his life and work will help the world to believe in a Divine Redeemer, and in the supernatural power of saving grace."

Secret Power was one of the earliest books published by D. L. Moody (1881). Within these pages, it should become clear that the anointing power, which attended the ministry of this man, was the Holy Spirit. Our earnest desire in republishing it as one of our Pure Gold Classics editions, is that each reader would be encouraged and inspired to "seek the Lord while he may be found" (Isa 55:6), and receive the power of His Spirit to live a holy life before God and man, sharing the truth of salvation unto all people.

May God richly bless this work unto His glory,

Gene Fedele
Editor

D.L. MOODY
1837-1899

Written by Rod Thomson

Flames of the inferno licked higher at the sky, feeding on the wooden city like a rabid beast. Emma Moody took their children to briefly look out the window at a city being destroyed—a sight few people have seen. Then they grabbed a small amount of belongings and fled in a wagon.

Her husband, D.L. Moody, was leaving an evening evangelistic meeting when he saw the horizon aglow. He knew instantly that it meant ruin for the great city of Chicago, and thus all of his physical work. The fire first reached Farwell Hall, which he had built four years earlier, then roared on to his Illinois Street Church and devoured it. No efforts of man could stem the destruction of the wind-whipped blaze. Finally, it consumed the Moody house along with most of their belongings.

Within a few days in October 1871, the worst fire in American history laid waste one of the great cities. But out of the ashes would grow a new and better city.

And out of the desolation of all his physical work, God would raise up a new and better worker in His servant, D.L. Moody.

At the behest of two devout women, Moody had been praying fervently for the Holy Spirit to be poured out on him that God might use him completely for the work of the Kingdom. This spiritual thirst continued after the fire. He provided comfort and help to many who lost everything in the fire. After a time, he went back east to raise money to begin rebuilding the church and public meeting place he knew was needed for evangelistic work. Because of his undisputed integrity, Moody could raise money like few men. But his heart wasn't in it. He was after God with everything in him.

In his own words:

"My heart was not in the work for begging. I could not appeal. I was crying all the time that God would fill me with His Spirit. Well, one day, in the City of New York – ah, what a day! —I cannot describe it, I seldom refer to it, it is almost too sacred an experience to name—Paul had an experience of which he never spoke for fourteen years—I can only say God revealed Himself to me, and I had such an experience of His love that I had to ask Him to stay His hand."

After this experience, Moody returned to preaching. He gave the same sermons, the same invitations, spoke the same way. But where before there was moderate interest in conversion to Christ, people now came in droves. Hundreds would fill inquiry rooms. Thousands upon thousands were saved in revivals in America and Europe.

The difference was not the servant, but the anointing God chose to place on the servant.

And Moody knew it.

"I should not now be placed back where I was before that blessed experience if you should give me all the world; it would be as the small dust of the balance."

Instead, the Lord used His servant to bring a substantial portion of the world to Him. He raised up a man who would lift Christ high, that all men might be drawn to Him. Here was a man of deep and committed faith in Christ, willing to give up a bright business future and his own pride in order to preach Christ to the lost.

Here was a man that God could use.

Knowing Poverty

Dwight Lyman Moody was raised about as poor in physical terms as a boy can be. Born Feb. 5, 1837 in Northfield, Mass., his father, Ed Moody, died when he was four years old, and the funeral was his earliest memory. The death left his mother, Betsy, a widow with seven children. A month after the funeral, she gave birth to twins. Nine boys, in all.

Materially, Dwight's life was one hardship after another. It was all he knew. His father died bankrupt and in debt. There were many who knew nothing of taking care of widows and orphans in their distress. In fact, creditors snatched everything from the household they could—including the widow's last kindling wood. On some cold, snowy mornings, she kept her children in bed until it was time to go to school because there was not wood for a fire to heat the house.

Many friends urged Betsy, who was a Unitarian at the time, to bind out some of her children to servitude, saying she could not raise them alone and that they would end up in jail. But she refused, and she pointed out later none of them ended up in jail. Dwight was always close to his mother, considering her his closest adult confidant after his wife. (She ultimately came forward at one of his crusades to accept Christ herself.)

At a very early age, Dwight hired himself out in the summer. His first job was to turn a neighbor's cows out to pasture. He earned a penny per day.

Dwight had a natural inclination toward practical jokes and everyone considered him fun to be around. He was known to play pranks, typically harmless, on about anyone—a part of his personality that continued all of his life. But there is no evidence that he had any particular inclination toward the things of God. Although his mother read the Bible and prayed, her Unitarian beliefs did not allow for faith in Christ for salvation. Dwight found church to be an excruciatingly boring exercise.

Boston Shoes

Moody did not enjoy farm work—although the farm never got fully out of him—and he had an ambitious streak in him. In 1854, at the age of 17, he went to Boston to work for his uncles in the boots and shoes business. Despite a lack of experience, he had natural salesman skills and excelled.

But in the plan of God, Boston turned out not to be about selling shoes. It was about Christ.

Moody was required to attend church and Sabbath-school (Sunday school) under the agreement to work for his uncles. This was a dry obligation until he was placed in the class of a godly man named Edward Kimball, who showed him kindness and love of the sort that made Moody very attentive in the class.

After a few months, on April 21, 1855, Kimball felt the need to speak to his new pupil about the condition of his soul. He found Moody at the shoe store wrapping up shoes in paper. Kimball very specifically laid out the love of Christ for him, and the sacrifice made for his salvation. Moody was suddenly ripe and as is so often the case, seeing Christ put everything else in a new perspective.

"The morning I was converted I went outdoors and fell in love with everything. I never loved the bright sun shining over the earth so much before. And when I heard the birds singing their sweet songs, I fell in love with the birds. Everything was different."

Indeed, the world would never be quite the same.

The Servant Begins

Moody moved to Chicago shortly after this, looking for the opportunities of what was then the West. Boston was too constrained and his ambition beckoned him to wide-open pastures.

His business acumen became more apparent as he entered the shoe business. Within a few years, he had saved $7,000, an enormous amount in those days. His self-confidence and optimism won him many friends, and his endless energy and strategic insights aided him in the business world, as it later would in the work of the eternal Kingdom. He told many people he planned to make $100,000, and few doubted he would.

During his first Sunday in Chicago, he went to the First Baptist Church's Sunday school, where his future wife attended as a young teen. He began attending the Plymouth Congregational Church and soon the zeal to share Christ took hold. He saw many lonely young men who did not attend church, particularly when the churches were so full. So he rented four pews and went out inviting men to sit with him. He immediately met with success.

He also joined the Young Men's Mission Band, distributing tracts and inviting people to church. On Sunday afternoons, he went to a small Sunday school. With such limited education—he went through the equivalent of fifth grade—he had no intention of teaching. But he felt he should offer to teach a class. The superintendent said they had more than enough teachers, but needed students. So the next Sunday, Moody arrived with 18 young men off the street—more than doubling the classes. He then began teaching them what little he knew at the time, and urging a decision for Christ.

In the fall of 1858, he began his own Sunday school class in a vacant saloon, aimed particularly at the boys of the streets. He had a soft heart of the hardships of fatherless children and young men. In no time, he required a larger building, as the young men were drawn to his simple but heart-felt message of Christ. The mayor even recognized the effort and provided a hall that was used for dancing and smoking Saturday nights. Moody, ever the willing servant, would arrive hours early at the hall and sweep out the cigar buttes and other garbage to prepare it for Sunday school.

John Farwell, a wealthy businessman who would become a close associate and benefactor for Moody's work, visited one Sunday. About half the class rushed to shine his shoes. But during the first meeting, Moody managed to get him named superintendent of the budding Sunday school.

A first principle of the classes was that the worse the boy was, the more argument there was against expelling him. Therefore, no one was ever kicked out.

Moody also was not shy about going into homes with the truth. In one case, he visited a woman whose husband would become violent when drinking. Moody took his jug of whiskey and dumped it out. When Moody returned to the house, the man, waiting for him, took his coat off to fight.

Moody said, "I emptied the jug for the good of yourself and your family. If I am to be thrashed for it, let me pray for you all before you do it." He then fell to his knees and fervently prayed for the man and his family. By the time he arose, the man was calmed and even allowed Moody to teach his children in Sunday school.

He was learning the powerful lessons of love. He once said, "Let love replace duty in our church relations, and the world will soon be evangelized."

Within several months of faithful, diligent work blessed of the Lord, the Sunday school classes contained 1,500 people, and this young, unknown, uneducated, poor-speaking man of God began to be recognized in the burgeoning city. Eventually, Presidents Lincoln and Grant would visit his Sunday schools in Chicago.

Another World

A dying teacher changed Moody's attitude toward business. The man's Sunday school class was full of silly young ladies. His lungs were bleeding, and he knew his time was limited. This humble man told Moody his greatest regret was that he had not led any of his Sunday school class to Christ and wondered if he had done more harm than good.

Moody had never heard that from anyone, and being the bold sort, he offered to take the man to the girls' homes to tell them his heart. As they did, girls who were previously trifling in all things broke down crying as the teacher told them of the love of Christ and state of their souls. He asked Moody to pray, and one by one, the girls sobbingly accepted Jesus until, by the following day, they had all stepped into the faith.

The man was returning to his home to die. Without any plan, all of the girls and Moody gathered at the train station with the dying teacher to see him off. They tried to sing, but broke down crying. The episode touched Moody deeply.

"The last we saw of that dying teacher he was standing on the platform in the rear of the car, his finger pointing upward, telling us to meet him in heaven." Moody knew in his heart that his business career was ended. "I didn't know what this was going to cost me. I was disqualified for business; it had become distasteful to me. I had got a taste of another world, and cared no more for making money."

This move made a tough choice for Emma Revell, to whom he was just recently engaged. To marry Moody now could mean a life of outright poverty. Yet not only did she love him, she carried a similar burden for lost souls. So she taught school for the three years of their engagement, and they were married in 1862, during the upheaval of the Civil War. It was a marriage that was perfect for Moody, for he had a wife who was a wonderful mother for his children, and a tireless aide in his ministry.

Moody's decision to leave business carried a sacrifice. All those people he had told that he planned to make $100,000 would now laugh at him. Coming from such poverty, he had set his sights on making plenty of money, and now he was giving that up. In his last eight months of business, he made $5,000. During his first year of working solely for the Lord, he made less than $300—voluntarily putting himself right back into the poverty from which he had just recently escaped. In all the decades of his ministry, he never received a regular salary from any source.

But he never looked back—his furrow was plowed straight. "God helped me to decide aright, and I have never regretted my choice."

To the Fields

The day that President Lincoln issued his call for soldiers to fight in the Civil War, Moody told a friend in his Sunday school: "We'll have to go, but we're here now. Let us do what we can to win a multitude of souls to Christ today."

In fact, while Moody was an abolitionist, he also was a pacifist based on Scripture, and he never took up arms in the war. Instead, he went to the Army camps, to the hospitals, and nine times to front-line battles to offer comfort to the troops and to preach Christ. God used him for a great many conversions of men whose lives probably turned out to be tragically shortened.

He was on the scene of the battles of Fort Donelson, Pittsburgh Landing, Shiloh and Murfreesboro. He arrived with the Army in Chattanooga and was one of the first into the shattered city of Richmond.

Whenever back in Chicago, the work of the Lord went on unabated. The converts to Jesus from his Sunday school class began multiplying to the point that Moody had problems knowing what to do with them all. He urged them to join several different churches, but the low, under-class of the city were uncomfortable in the large cathedrals with the upper classes.

The solution became the Illinois Street Church, which was built in 1864 for Sunday school and worship services. It held 1,500 people, and he preached Sunday mornings and taught 1,000 students Sunday afternoons. In keeping with his humble character, Moody made himself just one of the deacons. He eschewed all titles, even "reverend," in favor of "plain old Mr. Moody."

Moody won over a great many with unfeigned humbleness. He was one of several speakers at a Chicago convention when the minister following him criticized his grammar. Moody arose again when the man was done and thanked him, saying he knew he had great need in the area and asked the man to pray that God would help him improve his speech.

Two men and Moody signed a covenant with each other to pray and work for the building of a meeting hall for the Young Men's Christian Association, or YMCA. Unlike today, the YMCA at the time was very much focused on the "C." The YMCA aggressively distributed tracts and evangelized under Moody, who was president for two years. It became a strong force in the city.

Moody, who had just built the Illinois Street Church, led the way to construction of Farwell Hall, which he insisted be named after his friend and patron in the Lord's work. The building was dedicated in 1867 and Moody said during ceremonies that he believed the work in saving souls and attacking sin was barely begun. That was prophetically true. But there would be great trials. Four months after Farwell Hall was completed, it burned to the ground.

Undaunted, Moody set about raising money again and built a much better Farwell Hall this time. This hall was used for large meetings in which hundreds, perhaps thousands, were saved by Christ. But four years later, the building burned again, along with much of the city during the great Chicago fire that also swept away the church and Moody's home.

First Trip to Europe

The fire may have destroyed much of his work in Chicago, but God used it. The Lord chose to send spiritual fire into Moody's heart and anoint him to spark the fire of revival in much of the English-speaking world.

Moody had visited Europe in 1867 as his wife's doctor urged a sea trip for her chronic cough. Moody was not particularly interested in the rich history of Europe or the great edifices. But he did very much want to meet C. H. Spurgeon and George Mueller, both of whom had a large influence on the young American evangelist. Moody had learned much from the sermons of Spurgeon, and greatly admired the faith of Mueller running his orphanages without asking for money from man.

Moody was a virtual unknown in Europe on that trip, but he quickly distinguished himself in his typical self-deprecating, plain-speaking way. The leader of the Sunday school association in London was aware of Moody and asked him to speak at a meeting at Exeter Hall. Moody was introduced as "our American cousin, the Reverend Mr. Moody."

Moody arose and boldly set himself apart.

"The chairman has made two mistakes. To begin with, I'm not the 'reverend' Mr. Moody at all. I'm plain D.L. Moody, a Sabbath-school worker. And then I'm not your 'American cousin.' By the grace of God I'm your brother, who is interested, with you, in our Father's work for His children."

That left a hush in the hall, and yet Moody was quickly accepted by the English people, including the nobility—quite a different class than what he was accustomed to in Chicago. He became a close acquaintance with the reformer Lord Shaftsbury.

God's Team

Ira Sankey was earning a comfortable living working for the government in Pennsylvania when he met Moody at a YMCA convention in Indianapolis in 1870. Sankey, also an evangelist at heart, could sing like few men of his time, even though he had little training. And he was curious to hear this Moody speak.

One of the ministers urged Sankey to start off with a hymn before Moody began to speak. Without practice, Sankey arose and launched into "There is a fountain filled with blood, drawn from Immanuel's veins ..." The whole room joined in. After Moody spoke, Sankey was invited forward to meet Moody. Moody immediately recognized him as the man who had started the hymn, and took an intense interest in him.

The following exchange is one of those seminal moments that must be spelled out.

"Where are you from?" Moody asked, holding onto Sankey's hand.

"Pennsylvania," Sankey answered.

"Married?"

"Yes. I have a wife and two children."

"What do you do for a living when you are at home?"

"I am in the government service."

Moody continued gripping Sankey's hand tightly, and looked at him eye to eye. "Well, you'll have to give up business."

Sankey was stunned, silent and unsure what Moody was saying. So Moody went on. "You'll have to give up your government position, and come with me. You are the man I have been looking for the last eight years. I want you to come and help me in my work in Chicago."

Sankey was uncertain. He was not the man of bold vision that Moody was. He was no pioneer, and he held a very good job. He wavered over the next 24 hours, until Moody contacted him again, asking him if he would meet him that evening on a street corner to sing. Sankey agreed.

When Sankey arrived, Moody practically ignored him. He retrieved a large box from a nearby store, stood on it and asked Sankey to sing a hymn. After a couple of hymns, many people had gathered, and Moody began to preach. The crowd of mostly factory workers gathered even more. Sankey said later he had never heard such preaching. Moody jumped off the box and asked the crowd to follow him to a large hall, which they did as Sankey led them in "Shall We Gather at the River?" The hall filled quickly and Moody preached powerfully again. The throng was deeply moved.

Sankey had seen the future. He agreed to go to Chicago with Moody and history now inseparably links the names of Moody and Sankey.

It's clear that Moody's vision for using song to attract listeners and lift spirits was greatly realized in the God-given, euphonious voice of Ira Sankey.

Anointed for Revival

Filled with the Holy Spirit for the work of God, Moody set out for England with Sankey in 1873, with no expectations of what God was about to do. Both families went, but when they arrived they found that the two devoted Christian men who had invited them had died.

Moody chose not to move, but to wait on word from God. They got it when they received an invitation to speak in York. They accepted and began with small meetings. But between Moody's preaching and Sankey's hymns, the meetings grew and conversions quite suddenly mounted into the hundreds. They went on to other towns, with their reputation growing and the crowds getting larger.

God's hand was upon the work, and they were welcomed by all denominations, except the established Anglican Church. Since neither man was ordained, the established church refused to recognize them or their work, and that church was therefore bypassed. However, there is little doubt that many members of the church would ultimately attend the meetings.

Moody was invited to the large city of Edinburgh, Scotland. While there was a core greatly favoring Moody and Sankey, they had to overcome opposition. The Scottish were quite unaccustomed to Sankey's type of singing and to his organ, which many sincerely felt was an abomination. And Scottish clergymen were very staid and calm. Moody's fiery preaching was a sharp contrast. But his simplicity and sincerity won them, and the crowds in this big northern city were huge. The biggest building in use was unable to hold the throngs, and so meetings were held throughout the city.

It became clear that there was a powerful move of the Holy Spirit, and national newspapers began reporting on the "revival." This resurgence of the Spirit hit every class, from the highest aristocrats to the lowest street orphans. One prominent doctor stated that he believed every household in the city had been touched.

After three months, Moody moved on to Dundee for three months and then to Glasgow for four months. At a closing meeting in Glasgow, those converted at earlier meetings were invited. Nearly 4,000 people packed the hall.

Moody refused to keep track of any conversion numbers, declaring that was not his responsibility. When a doctor once asked him how many people were converted under his ministry, he said in his characteristic to-the-point fashion: "I don't know anything about that, Doctor. Thank God, I don't have to. I don't keep the Lamb's Book of Life."

The great Scottish revival moved on to Ireland with similar results and then flowed south to England's great cities like a snowball rolling downhill.

In 1875, Moody arrived in London for what would become one of the greatest evangelical campaigns in European history. The meetings were held at the Agricultural Hall, which could hold up to 20,000 people. Yet even that huge structure was completely insufficient for the crush of Londoners seeking God. Several other locations, seating up to 5,000 people, were also put into use and similarly swamped.

Biographer and Moody contemporary A.P. Fitt wrote: "Not only was London itself stirred, but the revival became a world-wide wonder."

Moody was no longer just a Chicago Sunday school teacher. At 38, after two years in Great Britain, God had raised up a humble world-wide evangelist the likes of which had never been seen there.

Fitt writes this summation of the English revival of 1873-75:

"Thousands of the unsaved and thousands of back-slidden Christians were led into a closer communion with God. A spirit of evangelism was awakened, and has never died down. A large number of city missions and other active aggressive organizations were established. Denominational differences were buried to a remarkable degree. Clergymen of all denominations were drawn into cooperation on a common platform, the salvation of the lost. Bibles were reopened, and Bible study received a wonderful impetus ... New life was infused into all methods of Christian activity. No attempt was made to proselytize, and converts were passed over to existing churches for nurture and admonition in the Lord."

Faithful with Money

Money was never an issue with Moody, and thus, it was never a source of attack. Once commissioned by God, he lost all interest in making it and largely all interest in what it could buy. His tastes were simple, and his mind and heart were always on the work of his Father.

The *New York Tribune* wrote of this issue following the English campaigns.

"There can be but one opinion as to the sincerity of Messrs. Moody and Sankey. They are not money-makers, they are not charlatans. Decorous, conservative England, which reprobated both their work and the manner of it, held them in the full blaze of scrutiny for months, and could not detect in them a single motive which was not pure."

This was grand praise from the secular media, even of that day.

There is a wonderful example of the kind of man Moody was with money, and it shows he associated himself with like-minded followers of Christ.

Moody had a vision for putting together a book of the hymns that were sung in the revival campaigns and putting them into as many hands as possible. But previous attempts at hymn books by publishers flopped. So Moody published his own and after they became popular, he found a publisher for larger blocks of books.

While in England for the great campaigns, the royalties on those hymn books began building up unknown to the men who were reaping out in the field. Finally the publishers contacted them and said there was $35,000 in their account. Now neither man had very much, and that was a veritable fortune in the 1870s. They sent word to the London committee of Christians they were working with that this amount was at their disposal for the work of the Lord. They simply turned over every penny. But a committee of fellow believers refused, saying it belonged to Moody and Sankey and that they would not accept such a large amount to *let* Moody preach. Their obvious feeling was that they should be giving something to Moody and Sankey.

Fitt notes the irony. "Here was a peculiar case—money going begging for want of a receiver." The money was eventually sent to Chicago to build a church.

Moody earned literally millions of dollars in his lifetime, and most of it passed through his hands for the work of the Lord in churches, schools, revivals, tracts and other activities he felt were right. In this way, he was very much like Mueller, whom he had such great respect for.

The Home Fires

Many great men of God through the centuries have struggled with the balance of their home lives. Often, they have felt the sting of a wayward or prodigal child. But

Moody's life in this respect was as solid as his evangelical work was spectacular.

Fitt wrote:

> "No man's private life will stand scrutiny better than D.L. Moody's, whether you consider him in the role of parent, neighbor, or friend. Always and throughout everything, he was a true Christian, a true man."

His marriage to Emma was blessed. They were one in the work of the Lord and one in the family. She was responsible for much of the raising of their three children: Emma, William and Paul. She also acted as his personal secretary for the decades of work in Chicago, Europe and across America. Whenever possible, which was much of the time, Moody would take his whole family with him on the campaigns. They were with him throughout the European campaigns, and on many American ones.

His children had only loving memories of their father and his "muscular Christianity." As an adult, his son Paul recalled his father as "the greatest man and the best man I have ever known."

While at the family home in Northfield, Moody discarded much of the trappings of the evangelist, particularly the warm, dark suit he always wore. He donned the farmer's comfortable clothing and set aside the work of the campaigns for periods.

He was popular in the town, not as a world-famous evangelist, but as a generous, honest, quick-witted man who opened his home to practically anyone, keeping them entertained with wonderful stories.

At times, Moody could act like a child who never quite grew up, particularly when he was with children. He easily reverted to the antics he was known for as a child. One of his sons remembered him as "a stout and bearded Peter Pan." His children had to be ready.

Once he dumped a bucket of water on some unsuspecting students at the Northfield school. Another time, he hid a deck of playing cards in his son's college room, acting astounded that his son would participate in such a heathen past time. Of course, Moody was very much against anything he considered time-wasting, and like many Christians in his day, he saw card-playing as akin to gambling.

"The devil tempts most men, but a lazy man tempts the devil," Moody told his children. "Don't wait for something to turn up. Go and turn up something."

He was tireless in his own servanthood for the Lord, and he taught his children likewise. "There is no use asking God to do things you can do yourself."

Moody transformed his little hometown. He established the Northfield Seminary for young women in 1879, the Mount Hermon School for young men in 1881, the Northfield Training School for young women in 1890 and the eastern depot for the Bible Institution's Colportage Association of Chicago in 1895. (This later became the Moody Bible Institute.)

To America and Back

Moody left for Europe a virtual unknown to the general American public. He returned to America a hero and as famous as any president. American newspapers had followed the English revival on a practically daily basis, and the coverage was quite positive.

He was ready to continue striking while the fire of the Holy Spirit was hot. Moody always thought strategically, almost like a battlefield commander. He understood the momentum of the moment, and so he made the decision to focus on the large cities.

"Cities are the centers of influence. Water runs downhill, and the highest hills in America are the great cities. If we can stir them we shall stir the whole country."

That was his desire, to see the gospel proclaimed in power from coast to coast. And so for the next three years he launched out on meetings for Christ in New York, Boston, Baltimore, Philadelphia, St. Louis, Cincinnati, Chicago and many other major cities. This effort, commencing in Brooklyn, resulted in a series of meetings that were unparalleled in the history of the country, both in the number of people attending and the number of lost sheep found by the Great Shepherd.

In New York, Moody preached in the Hippodrome, built by P.T. Barnum. The Hippodrome became the site of the original Madison Square Garden, where Billy Graham held his great New York crusades about 80 years later.

"To the Hippodrome!" became a rallying cry from the pulpit to the family hearth to the factory floor to the street corner. "To the Hippodrome!" fired the hearts of believers and attracted the non-believers in the droves. The Kingdom was charged during this period, as the revival fires spread wherever Moody and Sankey went, and continued long after they left.

In 1882, Moody was back in London for another campaign. In many respects, it was as though he picked up where he left off in 1876, as though he had never stopped. The huge crowds, new conversions and recommitments continued. Moody also began the practice of Saturday morning services for children, using illustrations to help them understand the gospel.

Upon his return, he went back to work in America, holding massive revival campaigns in the late 1880s and early 1890s. Denver, San Francisco, Richmond, Hartford, Providence and many others cities were added to the list of those touched by the tireless work of the evangelist. He had planned on traveling to India, China, New Zealand and Austria, but his health was failing him by the 1890s, and he was required to call off those trips. God would raise up others for that work.

To Higher Service

In his later years, Moody developed heart trouble, not a big surprise for a stocky man who constantly pushed himself. The doctors urged him to slow down and even stop many of his evangelistic endeavors. But he had a commission from God, and he would have none of it.

The Kansas City campaign in November 1899 would become his last. Although he arrived in Kansas City a sick man, he had preached six times in one day. During his final sermon, he spoke on the marriage supper of the bride and Bridegroom. There were two answers the listeners could give. They could deny the invitation, or they could write:

> "To the King of Heaven: While sitting in the Convention Hall, Kansas City, Mo., November 16, 1899, I received a pressing invitation from one of your messengers to be present at the marriage supper of your only-begotten Son. I hasten to reply. **By the Grace of God, I will be present."**

He pressed for the reply from those present, as he did whenever he spoke to a crowd. He urged commitment to Christ. But his illness became much worse, and he was forced to returned home before the Kansas City work was finished.

By the time he reached home, he had to be confined to his bed. The world was about to be stunned by Moody's sudden departure from this life, for very few people knew of his sickness.

On Dec. 22, he began his departure. It was slow, but almost painless. He lingered at the Jordan for many hours, giving those with him a glimpse of the other side.

"Earth recedes; heaven opens before me," he said at one point. "This is my triumph; this is my coronation day! I have been looking forward to it for years." His face suddenly lit up. "Dwight! Irene! I see the children's faces," he said of his two grandchildren who had died as youngsters.

Still, he lingered. He knew death was near and questioned the doctor who kept giving him medication that was only prolonging his family's suffering. He told Emma, whom he called "Mamma," that she had been a good wife to him.

Finally Moody's body succumbed to peace. He quietly fell asleep and his body sank down in the bed. But D.L. Moody was no longer in that broken old earthen jar. The good and faithful servant had moved on to behold the glorious face of Him whom he had served for more than four decades.

PHOTO GALLERY

Rev. D. L. Moody
1837-1899

BIRTHPLACE OF D.L. MOODY AT NORTHFIELD, MASS.

D.L. MOODY'S MOTHER. FROM A PORTRAIT TAKEN IN 1867.

DWIGHT L. MOODY AT THE TIME OF LEAVING HOME FOR BOSTON.

D.L. MOODY DURING EARLY YEARS IN CHICAGO.

MR. MOODY AT AGE 27: SUNDAY-SCHOOL WORKER.

MR. AND MRS. D.L. MOODY IN 1864 AND IN 1869.

HOME OF D.L. MOODY AT NORTHFIELD.

ILLINOIS STREET CHURCH, CHICAGO.
FIRST BUILDING ERECTED BY MR. MOODY. SCENE OF HIS EFFORTS
BEFORE THE CHICAGO FIRE.

MOODY'S TABERNACLE
FIRST BUILDING ERECTED AFTER THE CHICAGO FIRE. OCCUPIED FOR
TWO YEARS.

IRA D. SANKEY.

EXTERIOR OF OLD PENNSYLVANIA RAILROAD DEPOT, PHILADELPHIA.

INTERIOR OF OLD PENNSYLVANIA RAILROAD DEPOT, PHILADELPHIA.
SCENE OF THE GREAT MEETINGS IN PHILADELPHIA.

THE "HIPPODROME," NEW YORK

INTERIOR VIEW OF THE "HIPPODROME."
DURING THE NEW YORK MISSION.

IRA S. SANKEY (CENTER) ON THE PORCH OF BETSY MOODY
COTTAGE AT NORTHFIELD.

DELEGATES OF THE Y.M.C.A. ASSEMBLED IN CONVENTION AT NORTHFIELD.

Copyright 1900
Fleming H. Revell Co.

THE NORTHFIELD SEMINARY BUILDINGS, ON THE CONNECTICUT RIVER. MR. MOODY'S ENDURING MONUMENT.

INTERIOR OF THE MOODY AUDITORIUM AT NORTHFIELD.

MR. MOODY'S STUDY IN HIS HOME AT NORTHFIELD.

WITH CAMPERS AT CAMP NORTHFIELD.

New Birth

Most Solemn Question
that Will Ever
Come before us in
this life

The foundation of
All our Hopes in the
life to Come

It is the A. B. C
of our Blessed
Hope

SERMON NOTES IN MOODY'S OWN HAND.

Nothing will up
Set-false religion
like it

It will Change
Our thoughts about
God the Bible Sooner
than anything Else

I Believe it is the
Greatest Blessing
that will Ever Come
to us in this life

MR. MOODY HAILING A FRIEND.

MOODY WITH DAUGHTER AND GRANDAUGHTER.

MR. MOODY AS HIS TOWNSFOLK KNEW HIM.

MR. AND MRS. MOODY WITH GRANDCHILDREN.

ABSORBED IN HIS CORRESPONDENCE.

MR. MOODY AS HE APPEARED IN 1886.

BIBLE USED BY MR. MOODY FOR MANY YEARS.

R. A. Torrey

Why God Used D. L. Moody

by R. A. Torrey (Written in 1923)

Eighty-six years ago (February 5, 1837), there was born of poor parents in a humble farmhouse in Northfield, Massachusetts, a little baby who I believe was to become the greatest man of his generation or of his century—Dwight L. Moody. After our great generals, great statesmen, great scientists and great men of letters have passed away and been forgotten, and their work and its helpful influence has come to an end, the work of D. L. Moody will go on and its saving influence continue and increase, bringing blessing not only to every state in the Union but to every nation on earth. Yes, it will continue throughout the ages of eternity.

My subject is "Why God Used D. L. Moody," and I can think of no subject upon which I would rather speak. For I shall not seek to glorify Mr. Moody, but the God who by His grace, His entirely unmerited favor, used him so mightily, and the Christ who saved him by His atoning death and resurrection life, and the Holy Ghost who lived in him and wrought through him and who alone made him the mighty power that he was to this world. Furthermore, I hope to make it clear that the God who used D. L. Moody in his day is just as ready to use you and me in this day if we, on our part, do what D. L. Moody did, which was what made it possible for God to so abundantly use him.

The whole secret of why D. L. Moody was such a mightily used man you will find in Psalm 62:11, "God hath spoken once; twice have I heard this; that POWER BELONGETH UNTO GOD." I am glad it does. I am glad that power did not belong to D. L. Moody. I am glad that it did not belong to Charles G. Finney. I am glad that it did not belong to Martin Luther. I am glad that it did not belong to any other Christian man [or woman] whom God has greatly used in this world's history. Power belongs to God. If D. L. Moody had any power, and he had great power, he got it from God.

But God does not give His power arbitrarily. It is true that He gives it to whomsoever He will, but He wills to give it on certain conditions, which are clearly revealed in His Word. D. L. Moody met those conditions, and God made him the most wonderful preacher of his generation. Yes, I think the most wonderful man of his generation.

But how was it that D. L. Moody had that power of God so wonderfully manifested in his life? Pondering this question, it seemed to me that there were seven things in the life of D. L. Moody that accounted for God's using him so largely as He did.

1. A Fully Surrendered Man

The first thing that accounts for God using D. L. Moody so mightily was that he was a fully surrendered man. Every ounce of that two-hundred-and-eighty -pound body of his belonged to God. Everything he was and everything he had belonged wholly to God. Now, I am not saying that Mr. Moody was perfect. He was not. If I attempted to, I presume I could point out some defects in his character. It does not occur to me at this moment what they were. But I am confident that I could think of some, if I tried real hard. I have never yet met a perfect man, not one. I have known perfect men in the sense in which the Bible commands us to be perfect, i.e., men who are wholly God's, out and out for God, fully surrendered to God, with no will but God's will. But I have never known a man in whom I could not see some defects, some places where he might have been improved.

No, Mr. Moody was not a faultless man. If he had any flaws in his character, and he did, I was in a position to know them better than almost any other man because of my very close association with him in the later years of his life. Furthermore, I suppose that in his latter days he opened his heart to me more fully than to anyone else in the world. I think He told me some things that he told no one else. So I presume I knew whatever defects there were in his character as well as anybody. But while I recognized such flaws, I know that he was a man who belonged wholly to God.

The first month I was in Chicago, we were having a talk about something upon which we very widely differed, and Mr. Moody turned to me very frankly and very kindly and said in defense of his own position, "Torrey, if I believed that God wanted me to jump out of that window, I would jump." I believe he would. If he thought God wanted him to do anything, he would do it. He belonged wholly, unreservedly, unqualifiedly, entirely, to God.

51

Henry Varley, a very intimate friend of Mr. Moody in the earlier days of his work, loved to tell how he once said to him, "It remains to be seen what God will do with a man who gives himself up wholly to Him."

I am told that when Mr. Henry Varley said that, Mr. Moody said to himself, "Well, I will be that man." And I, for my part, do not think "it remains to be seen" what God will do with a man who gives himself up wholly to Him. I think it has been seen already in D. L. Moody.

If you and I are to be used in our sphere as D. L. Moody was used in his, we must put all that we have and all that we are in the hands of God, for Him to use as He will, to send us where He will, for God to do with us what He will, and we, on our part, to do everything God bids us do.

There are thousands and tens of thousands of men and women in Christian work, brilliant men and women, rarely gifted men and women, men and women who are making great sacrifices, men and women who have put all conscious sin out of their lives. Yet many of them have stopped short of absolute surrender to God, and therefore have stopped short of fullness of power. But Mr. Moody did not stop short of absolute surrender to God, he was a wholly surrendered man. And if you and I are to be used, you and I must be wholly surrendered men and women.

2. A Man of Prayer

The second secret of the great power exhibited in Mr. Moody's life was that Mr. Moody was in the deepest and most meaningful sense a man of prayer. People oftentimes say to me, "Well, I went many miles to see and to hear D.

L. Moody and he certainly was a wonderful preacher." Yes, D. L. Moody certainly was a wonderful preacher. Taking it all in all, the most wonderful preacher I have ever heard, and it was a great privilege to hear him preach as he alone could preach. But out of a very intimate acquaintance with him I wish to testify that he was far greater at praying than he was at preaching.

Time and time again, he was confronted by obstacles that seemed insurmountable, but he always knew the way to surmount and to overcome all difficulties. He knew the way to bring to pass anything that needed to be brought to pass. He knew and believed in the deepest depths of his soul that "nothing was too hard for the Lord," and that prayer could do anything that God could do.

Often times Mr. Moody would write me when he was about to undertake some new work, saying, "I am beginning work in such and such a place on such and such a day. I wish you would get the students together for a day of fasting and prayer."

And often I have taken those letters and read them to the students in the lecture room and said, "Mr. Moody wants us to have a day of fasting and prayer, first for God's blessing on our own souls and work, and then for God's blessing on him and his work."

Many times we were gathered in the lecture room far into the night—sometimes until one, two, three, four, or even five o'clock in the morning, crying to God, just because Mr. Moody urged us to wait upon God until we received His blessing. How many men and women I have known whose lives and characters have been transformed by those nights of prayer and who have wrought mighty things in many lands because of them!

One day Mr. Moody drove up to my house at Northfield and said, "Torrey, I want you to take a ride with me." I got into the carriage and we drove out toward Morgan's Lane, talking about some great and unexpected difficulties that had arisen in regard to the work in Northfield and Chicago, and in connection with other work that was very dear to him.

As we drove along, some black storm clouds lay ahead of us, and then suddenly, as we were talking, it began to rain. He drove the horse into a shed near the entrance to Morgan's Lane to shelter the horse, and then laid the reins upon the dashboard and said, "Torrey, pray." I prayed as best I could, while he in his heart joined me in prayer. And when my voice was silent he began to pray. Oh, I wish you could have heard that prayer! I shall never forget it, so simple, so trustful, so definite, so direct, and so mighty. When the storm was over and we drove back to town, the obstacles had been surmounted, and the work of the schools, and other work that was threatened, went on as it had never gone on before, and it has gone on until this day.

As we drove back, Mr. Moody said to me: "Torrey, we will let the other men do the talking and the criticizing, and we will stick to the work that God has given us to do, and let Him take care of the difficulties and answer the criticisms."

On one occasion Mr. Moody said to me in Chicago, "I have just found, to my surprise, that we are twenty thousand dollars behind in our finances for the work here and in Northfield, and we must have that twenty thousand dollars, and I am going to get it by prayer." He did not tell a soul who had the ability to give a penny of the twenty thousand dollars' deficit, but looked right to God and said, "I need twenty thousand dollars for my work—send me that money in such a way that I will know it comes straight from Thee." And God heard that prayer. The money came in such a way that it was clear that it came from God in direct answer to prayer.

Yes, D. L. Moody was a man who believed in the God who answers prayer, and not only believed in Him in a theoretical way but believed in Him in a practical way. He was a man who met every difficulty that stood in his way—by prayer. Everything he undertook was backed up by prayer, and in everything his ultimate dependence was upon God.

3. A Deep and Practical Student of the Bible

The third secret of Mr. Moody's power, or the third reason why God used D. L. Moody, was because he was a deep and practical student of the Word of God. Nowadays it is often said of D. L. Moody that he was not a student. I wish to say that he was a student. Most emphatically he was a student. He was not a student of psychology, he was not a student of anthropology—I am very sure he would not have known what that word meant. He was not a student of biology, he was not a student of philosophy, he was not even a student of theology in the technical sense of the term. But he was a student, a profound and practical student, of the one book that is more worth studying than all other books in the world put together—he was a student of the Bible.

Every day of his life, I have reason for believing, he arose very early in the morning to study the Word of God, down to the very close of his life. Mr. Moody used to rise about four o'clock in the morning to study the Bible. He would say to me, "If I am going to get in any study, I have got to get up before the other folks get up." Each morning he would shut himself up in a remote room in his house, alone with his God and his Bible.

I shall never forget the first night I spent in his home. He had invited me to take the Superintendency of the Bible Institute and I had already begun my work. I was on my way to some city in the East to preside at the International Christian Workers' Convention. He wrote me saying: "Just as soon as the Convention is over, come up to Northfield." He learned when I was likely to arrive and drove over to South Vernon to meet me. That night he had all the teachers from the Mount Hermon School and from the Northfield Seminary come together at the house to meet me, and to talk over the problems of the two schools. We talked together far on into the night, and then, after the principals and teachers of the schools had gone home, Mr. Moody and I talked together about the problems a while longer.

It was very late when I got to bed that night, but very early the next morning, about five o'clock, I heard a gentle tap on my door. Then I heard Mr. Moody's voice whispering, "Torrey, are you up?" I happened to be—I do not always get up at that early hour but I happened to be up that particular morning. He said, "I want you to go somewhere with me," and I went down with him. Then I found out that he had already been up an hour or two in his room studying the Word of God.

You may talk about power, but if you neglect the one book that God has given you as the one instrument through which He imparts and exercises His power, you will not have it. You may read many books and go to many conventions and you may have your all-night prayer meetings to pray for the power of the Holy Ghost, but unless you keep in constant and close association with the Bible you will not have power. And if you ever had power, you will not maintain it except by the daily, earnest, intense, study of that Book.

Ninety-nine Christians in every hundred are merely playing at Bible study, and therefore ninety-nine Christians in every hundred are mere weaklings when they might be giants, both in their Christian life and in their service.

It was largely because of his thorough knowledge of the Bible, and his practical knowledge of the Bible, that Mr. Moody drew such immense crowds. On "Chicago Day" in October, 1893, none of the theaters of Chicago dared to open because it was expected that everybody in Chicago would go on that day to the World's Fair. In point of fact, something like four-hundred-thousand people did pass through the gates of the Fair that day. Everybody in Chicago was expected to be at that end of the city on that day. But Mr. Moody said to me, "Torrey, engage the Central Music Hall and announce meetings from nine o'clock in the morning until six o'clock at night."

"Why," I replied, "Mr. Moody, nobody will be at this end of Chicago on that day. Not even the theaters dare to open. Everybody is going down to Jackson Park to the Fair. We cannot get anybody out on this day."

Mr. Moody replied: "You do as you are told."

I did as I was told and engaged the Central Music Hall for continuous meetings from nine o'clock in the morning until six o'clock at night. But I did it with a heavy heart. I thought there would be poor audiences. I was on the program at noon that day. Being very busy in my office about the details of the campaign, I did not reach the Central Music Hall until almost noon. I thought I would have no trouble in getting in. But when I got almost to the Hall I found to my amazement that not only was it packed, but the vestibule was packed, and the steps were packed, and there was no getting anywhere near the door. If I had not gone round and climbed in a back window they would have lost their speaker for that hour.

But that would not have been of much importance, for the crowds had not gathered to hear me. It was the magic of Mr. Moody's name that had drawn them. And why did they long to hear Mr. Moody? Because they knew that while he was not versed in many of the philosophies and fads and fancies of the day, he did know the one book that this old world most longs to know—the Bible.

I shall never forget Moody's last visit to Chicago. The ministers of Chicago had sent me to Cincinnati to invite him to come to Chicago and hold a meeting. In response to the invitation, Mr. Moody said to me, "If you will hire the Auditorium for weekday mornings and afternoons and have meetings at ten in the morning and three in the afternoon, I will go."

I replied, "Mr. Moody, you know what a busy city Chicago is, and how impossible it is for businessmen to get out at ten o'clock in the morning and three in the afternoon on working days. Will you not hold evening meetings and meetings on Sunday?"

"No," he replied, "I am afraid if I did, I would interfere with the regular work of the churches."

I went back to Chicago and engaged the Auditorium, which at that time was the building having the largest seating capacity of any building in the city, seating in those days about seven thousand people. I announced weekday meetings, with Mr. Moody as the speaker at ten o'clock in the mornings and three o'clock in the afternoons.

At once protests began to pour in upon me. One of them came from Marshall Field, at that time the business king of Chicago. "Mr. Torrey," Mr. Field wrote, "we businessmen of Chicago wish to hear Mr. Moody, and you know perfectly well how impossible it is for us to get out at ten o'clock in the morning and three o'clock in the afternoon. Have evening meetings."

I received many letters of a similar nature and wrote to Mr. Moody urging him to give us evening meetings. But Mr. Moody simply replied, "You do as you are told," and I did as I was told—that is the way I kept my job.

On the first morning of the meetings I went down to the Auditorium about half an hour before the appointed time, but I went with much fear and apprehension. I thought the Auditorium would be nowhere near full. When I reached there, I found to my amazement a line of people four abreast extending from the Congress Street entrance to Wabash Avenue, then a block north on Wabash Avenue, then a break to let traffic through, and then another block, and so on. I went in through the back door, and there were many clamoring for entrance there.

When the doors were opened at the appointed time, we had a cordon of twenty policemen to keep back the crowd. But the crowd was so great that it swept the cordon of policemen off their feet and packed eight thousand people into the building before we could get the doors shut. And I think there were as many left on the outside as there were in the building. I do not think that anyone else in the world could have drawn such a crowd at such a time.

Why? Because though Mr. Moody knew little about science or philosophy or literature in general, he did know the one book that this old world is perishing to know and longing to know. And this old world will flock to hear men [and women] who know the Bible and preach the Bible, as they will flock to hear nothing else on earth.

During all the months of the World's Fair in Chicago, no one could draw such crowds as Mr. Moody. Judging by the papers, one would have thought that the great religious event in Chicago at that time was the World's Congress of Religions [that was also being held]. One very gifted man of letters in the East was invited to speak at this Congress. He saw in this invitation the opportunity of his life and prepared his paper, the exact title of which I do not now recall, but it was something along the line of "New Light on the Old Doctrines." He prepared the paper with great care, and then sent it around to his most trusted and gifted friends for criticisms. These men sent it back to him with such changes as they had to suggest. Then he rewrote the paper, incorporating as many of the suggestions and criticisms as seemed wise. Then he sent it around for further criticisms. Then he wrote the paper a third time, and had it, as he trusted, perfect. He went on to Chicago to meet this coveted opportunity of speaking at the World's Congress of Religions.

It was at eleven o'clock on a Saturday morning (if I remember correctly) that he was to speak. He stood outside the door of the platform waiting for the great moment to arrive, and as the clock struck eleven he walked on to the platform to face a magnificent audience of eleven women and two men! But there was not a building anywhere in Chicago that would accommodate the very same day the crowds that would flock to hear Mr. Moody at any hour of the day or night.

Oh, men and women, if you wish to get an audience and wish to do that audience some good after you get them, study, study, STUDY the one book, and preach, preach, PREACH the one book, and teach, teach, TEACH the one book—the Bible. It's the only book that is God's Word, and the only book that has power to gather and hold and bless the crowds for any great length of time.

4. A Humble Man

The fourth reason why God continuously used D.L. Moody through so many years was because he was a humble man. I think D. L. Moody was the humblest man I ever knew in all my life. He loved to quote the words of another: "Faith gets the most, love works the most, but humility keeps the most."

He himself had the humility that keeps everything it gets. As I have already said, he was the most humble man I ever knew; i.e., the most humble man when we bear in mind the great things that he did, and the praise that was lavished upon him. Oh, how he loved to put himself in the background and put other men in the foreground. How often he would stand on a platform with some of us little fellows seated behind him and as he spoke he would say, "There are better men coming after me." As he said it, he would point back over his shoulder with his thumb to the "little fellows." I do not know how he could believe it, but he really did believe that the others that were coming after him were better than he was. He made no pretense to a humility he did not possess. In his heart of hearts he constantly underestimated himself, and overestimated others.

He really believed that God would use other men in a larger measure than he had been used. Mr. Moody loved to keep himself in the background. At his conventions at Northfield, or anywhere else, he would push the other men to the front and, if he could, have them do all the preaching—McGregor, Campbell Morgan, Henry Drummond, Andrew Murray, and the rest of them. The only way we could get him to take any part in the program was to get up in the convention and move that we hear D. L. Moody at the next meeting. He continually put himself out of sight.

How many a man has been full of promise and God has used him, and then the man thought that he was the whole thing and God was compelled to set him aside. I believe more promising workers have gone on the rocks through self-sufficiency and self-esteem than through any other cause. I can look back for forty years or more, and think of many men who are now wrecks or derelicts who at one time the world thought were going to be something great. But they have disappeared entirely from the public view. Why? Because of overestimation of self. There have been numerous men and women put aside because they began to think that they were somebody, that they were "IT," and therefore God was compelled to set them aside.

WHY GOD USED D. L. MOODY

I remember a man with whom I was closely associated in a great movement in this country. We were having a most successful convention in Buffalo, and he was greatly elated. As we walked down the street together to one of the meetings one day, he said to me, "Torrey, you and I are the most important men in Christian work in this country," or words to that effect.

I replied, "John, I am sorry to hear you say that, for as I read my Bible I find man after man who had accomplished great things whom God had to set aside because of his sense of his own importance." And God set that man aside also from that time. I think he is still living, but no one ever hears of him, or has heard of him for years.

God used D. L. Moody, I think, beyond any man of his day, but it made no difference how much God used him, he never was puffed up. One day, speaking to me of a great New York preacher, now dead, Mr. Moody said, "He once did a very foolish thing, the most foolish thing that I ever knew a man, ordinarily so wise as he was, to do. He came up to me at the close of a little talk I had given and said, 'Young man, you have made a great address tonight.'" Then Mr. Moody continued, "How foolish of him to have said that. It almost turned my head." But, thank God, it did not turn his head, and even when most of the ministers in England, Scotland, and Ireland, and many of the English bishops, were ready to follow D. L. Moody wherever he led, even then it never turned his head one bit. He would get down on his face before God, knowing he was human, and ask God to empty him of all self-sufficiency. And God did.

Oh, men and women! especially young men and young women, perhaps God is beginning to use you. If so, it's very likely people are saying: "What a wonderful gift he has as a Bible teacher, what power he has as a preacher, for such a young man!" Listen—get down upon your face before God. I believe here lies one of the most dangerous snares of the Devil. When the Devil cannot discourage a man, he approaches him on another tack, which he knows is far worse in its results—he puffs him up by whispering in his ear, "You are the leading evangelist of the day. You are the man who will sweep everything before you. You are the coming man. You are the D. L. Moody of the day." And if you listen to him, he will ruin you. The entire shore of the history of Christian workers is strewn with the wrecks of gallant vessels that were full of promise a few years ago, but these men became puffed up and were driven on the rocks by the wild winds of their own raging self-esteem.

5. His Entire Freedom from the Love of Money

The fifth secret of D. L. Moody's continual power and usefulness was his entire freedom from the love of money. Mr. Moody might have been a wealthy man, but money had no charms for him. He loved to gather money for God's work, but he refused to accumulate money for himself. He told me during the World's Fair that if he had taken for himself the royalties on the hymnbooks that he had published, they would have amounted, at that time, to a million dollars. But Mr. Moody refused to touch the money. He had a perfect right to take it, for he was responsible for the publication of the books and it was his money that went into the publication of the first of them.

Mr. Sankey had some hymns that he had taken with him to England and he wished to have them published. He went to a publisher (I think Morgan & Scott) and they declined to publish them, because, as they said, Philip Phillips had recently been over and published a hymnbook and it had not done well. Mr. Moody, however, had a little money and he said that he would put it into the publication of these hymns in cheap form, and he did. The hymns had a most remarkable and unexpected sale. They were then published in book form and large profits accrued. The financial results were offered to Mr. Moody, but he refused to touch them. "But," it was urged on him, "the money belongs to you." Nevertheless, he would not touch it.

Mr. Fleming H. Revell was at the time treasurer of the Chicago Avenue Church, commonly known as the Moody Tabernacle. Only the basement of this new church building had been completed, funds having been exhausted. Hearing of the hymnbook situation Mr. Revell suggested, in a letter to friends in London, that the money be given for completion of this building, and it was. Afterwards, so much money came in that it was given, by the committee into whose hands Mr. Moody put the matter, to various Christian enterprises.

In a certain city to which Mr. Moody went in the latter years of his life, and where I went with him, it was publicly announced that Mr. Moody would accept no money whatever for his services. Now, in point of fact, Mr. Moody was dependent, in a measure, upon what was given him at various services. But when this announcement was made, Mr. Moody said nothing, and left that city without a penny's compensation for the hard work he did there. I think he even paid his own hotel bill. And yet a minister in that very city came out with an article in a paper, which I read, in which he told a fairy tale of the financial demands that Mr. Moody made upon them. It was a story that I knew personally to be absolutely untrue. Millions of dollars passed into Mr. Moody hands, but they passed through; they did not stick to his fingers.

This is the point at which many an evangelist makes shipwreck, and his great work comes to an untimely end. The love of money on the part of some evangelists has done more to discredit evangelistic work in our day, and to lay many an evangelist on the shelf, than almost any other cause.

While I was away on my recent tour I was told by one of the most reliable ministers in one of our eastern cities of a campaign conducted by one who has been greatly used in the past. (Do not imagine, for a moment, that I am speaking of Billy Sunday, for I am not. This same minister spoke in the highest terms of Mr. Sunday and of a campaign which he conducted in a city where this minister was a pastor.) This evangelist of whom I now speak came to a city for a united evangelistic campaign and was supported by fifty-three churches. The minister who told me about the matter was himself chairman of the Finance Committee.

The evangelist showed such a longing for money and so deliberately violated the agreement he had made before coming to the city and so insisted upon money being gathered for him in other ways than he had himself prescribed in the original contract, that this minister threatened to resign from the Finance Committee. He was, however, persuaded to remain to avoid a scandal.

"The total result of the three weeks' campaign was that there were only twenty-four clear decisions [salvations]," said my friend. "After it was over the ministers got together and by a vote, with but one dissenting voice, agreed to send a letter to this evangelist telling him frankly that they were done with him and with his methods of evangelism forever, and that they felt it their duty to warn other cities against him and his methods and the results of his work." Let us lay the lesson to our hearts and take warning in time.

6. His Consuming Passion for the Salvation of the Lost

The sixth reason why God used D. L. Moody was because of his consuming passion for the salvation of the lost. Shortly after he was saved, Mr. Moody made the resolution that he would never let twenty-four hours pass over his head without speaking to at least one person about his soul. His was a very busy life, and sometimes he would forget his resolution until the last hour, and sometimes he would get out of bed, dress, and go out and talk to someone about his soul in order that he might not let one day pass without having definitely told at least one of his fellow-mortals about his need and the Savior who could meet it.

One night Mr. Moody was going home from his place of business. It was very late, and it suddenly occurred to him that he had not spoken to one single person that day about accepting Christ. He said to himself, "Here's a day lost. I have not spoken to anyone today and I shall not see anybody at this late hour." But as he walked up the street he saw a man standing under a lamppost. The man was a perfect stranger to him, though it turned out afterwards the man knew who Mr. Moody was. He stepped up to this stranger and said, "Are you a Christian?"

The man replied: "That is none of your business, whether I am a Christian or not. If you were not a sort of a preacher I would knock you into the gutter for your impertinence." Mr. Moody said a few earnest words and passed on.

The next day that man called upon one of Mr. Moody's prominent business friends and said to him: "That man Moody of yours over on the North Side is doing more harm than he is good. He has got zeal without knowledge. He stepped up to me last night, a perfect stranger, and insulted me. He asked me if I were a Christian, and I told him it was none of his business and if he were not a sort of a preacher I would knock him into the gutter for his impertinence. He is doing more harm than he is good. He has got zeal without knowledge."

Mr. Moody's friend sent for him and said: "Moody, you are doing more harm than you are good. You've got zeal without knowledge. You insulted a friend of mine on the street last night. You went up to him, a perfect stranger, and asked him if he were a Christian, and he tells me if you had not been a sort of a preacher he would have knocked you into the gutter for your impertinence. You are doing more harm than you are good. You have got zeal without knowledge."

Mr. Moody went out of that man's office somewhat crestfallen. He wondered if he were not doing more harm than he was good, if he really had zeal without knowledge. (Let me say, in passing, it is far better to have zeal without knowledge than it is to have knowledge without zeal. Some men and women are as full of knowledge as an egg is of meat. They are so deeply versed in Bible truth that they can sit in criticism on the preachers and give the preachers pointers, but they have so little zeal that they do not lead one soul to Christ in a whole year.)

Weeks passed by. One night Mr. Moody was in bed when he heard a tremendous pounding at his front door. He jumped out of bed and rushed to the door. He thought the house was on fire. He thought the man would break down the door. He opened the door and there stood this man. He said, "Mr. Moody, I have not had a good night's sleep since that night you spoke to me under the lamppost, and I have come around at this unearthly hour of the night for you to tell me what I have to do to be saved." Mr. Moody took him in and told him what to do to be saved. Then he accepted Christ, and when the Civil War broke out, he went to the front and laid down his life fighting for his country.

Another night, Mr. Moody got home and had gone to bed before it occurred to him that he had not spoken to a soul that day about accepting Christ. "Well," he said to himself, "it is no good getting up now, there will be nobody on the street at this hour of the night." But he got up anyway, dressed, and went to the front door. It was pouring rain. "Oh," he said, "there will be no one out in this pouring rain."

Just then he heard the patter of a man's feet as he came down the street, holding an umbrella over his head. Mr. Moody darted out and rushed up to the man and said, "May I share the shelter of your umbrella?"

"Certainly," the man replied.

Then Mr. Moody said, "Have you any shelter in the time of storm?" and preached Jesus to him. Oh, men and women, if we were as full of zeal for the salvation of souls as that, how long would it be before the whole country would be shaken by the power of a mighty God-sent, Holy Ghost, revival?

One day in Chicago—the day after the elder Carter Harrison was shot and his body was lying in state in the City Hall—Mr. Moody and I were riding up Randolph Street together in a streetcar right alongside of the City Hall. The car could scarcely get through because of the enormous crowds waiting to get in and view the body of Mayor Harrison. As the car tried to push its way through the crowd, Mr. Moody turned to me and said, "Torrey, what does this mean?"

"Why," I said, "Carter Harrison's body lies there in the City Hall and these crowds are waiting to see it."

Then he said, "This will never do, to let these crowds get away from us without preaching to them. We must talk to them. You go and hire Hooley's Opera House (which was just opposite the City Hall) for the whole day." I did so. The meetings began at nine o'clock in the morning, and we had one continuous service from that hour until six in the evening, to reach those crowds.

Mr. Moody was a man on fire for God. Not only was he always "on the job" himself, but he was always getting others to work as well. He once invited me down to Northfield to spend a month there with the schools, speaking first to one school and then crossing the river to the other. I was obliged to use the ferry a great deal because it was before the present bridge was built at that point.

One day Moody said to me, "Torrey, did you know that that ferryman that ferries you across every day is unconverted?" He did not tell me to speak to him, but I knew what he meant. When some days later it was told him that the ferryman was saved, he was exceedingly happy.

Once, when walking down a certain street in Chicago, Mr. Moody stepped up to a man, a perfect stranger to him, and said: "Sir, are you a Christian?"

"You mind your own business," was the reply.

Mr. Moody said, "This is my business."

The man said, "Well, then, you must be Moody."

In those early days in Chicago they used to call him "Crazy Moody," because day and night he was speaking to everybody he got a chance to speak to about being saved. One time he was going to Milwaukee, and in the seat that he had chosen sat a traveling man [traveling salesman]. Mr. Moody sat down beside him and immediately began to talk with him. " Where are you going?" Mr. Moody asked. When told the name of the town he said: "We will soon be there so we'll have to get down to business at once. Are you saved?" The man said that he was not, and Mr. Moody took out his Bible and there on the train showed him the way of salvation. Then he said: "Now, you must take Christ." The man did and he was converted right there on the train.

Most of you have heard, I presume, the story President Wilson used to tell about D. L. Moody. Ex-President Wilson said that he once went into a barber shop and took a chair next to the one in which D. L. Moody was sitting, though he did not know that Mr. Moody was there. He had not been in the chair very long before, as ex-President Wilson phrased it, he "knew there was a personality in the other chair," and he began to listen to the conversation going on. He heard Mr. Moody tell the barber about the Way of Life, and President Wilson said, "I have never forgotten that scene to this day." When Mr. Moody was gone, he asked the barber who he was. When he was told that it was D. L. Moody, President Wilson said, "It made an impression upon me I have not yet forgotten."

On one occasion in Chicago, Mr. Moody saw a little girl standing on the street with a pail in her hand. He went up to her and invited her to his Sunday school, telling her what a pleasant place it was. She promised to go the following Sunday, but she did not do so. Mr. Moody watched for her for weeks, and then one day he saw her on the street again, at some distance from him. He started toward her, but she saw him and started to run away. Mr. Moody followed her.

Down she went one street, Mr. Moody after her; up she went another street, Mr. Moody after her; through an alley, Mr. Moody still following. They came out on another street with Mr. Moody right after her. Then she dashed into a saloon and Mr. Moody dashed after her. She ran out the back door and up a flight of stairs, Mr. Moody still following. She dashed into a room, Mr. Moody following. She threw herself under the bed and Mr. Moody reached under the bed and pulled her out by the foot, and led her to Christ.

He found that her mother was a widow who had once seen better circumstances, but had gone down until now she was living over this saloon. She had several children. Mr. Moody led the mother and all the family to Christ. Several of the children were prominent members of the Moody Church until they moved away, and afterwards became prominent in churches elsewhere. This particular child, whom he pulled from underneath the bed, was, when

I was the pastor of the Moody Church, the wife of one of the most prominent officers in the church.

Only two or three years ago, as I came out of a ticket office in Memphis, Tennessee, a fine-looking young man followed me. He said: "Are you not Dr. Torrey?"

I said, "Yes."

He said, "I am so and so." He was the son of this woman. He was then a traveling man, and an officer in the church where he lived. When Mr. Moody pulled that little child out from under the bed by the foot, he was pulling a whole family into the Kingdom of God, and eternity alone will reveal how many succeeding generations he was pulling into the Kingdom of God.

D.L. Moody's consuming passion for souls was not for the souls of those who would be helpful to him in building up his work here or elsewhere. His love for souls knew no class limitations. He was no respecter of persons. It might be an earl or a duke or it might be an ignorant boy on the street. It was all the same to him. There was a soul to save and he did what lay in his power to save that soul.

A friend once told me that the first time he ever heard of Mr. Moody was when Mr. Reynolds of Peoria told him that he once found Mr. Moody sitting in one of the squatters' shanties that used to be in that part of the city toward the lake, which was then called "The Sands." Mr. Moody had a young boy on his knee, a tallow candle in one hand, and a Bible in the other, and he was spelling out the words (the boy could not read very well) of certain verses of Scripture, in an attempt to lead that ignorant boy to Christ.

Oh, young men and women and all Christian workers, if you and I were on fire for souls like that, how long would it be before we had a revival? What would happen if tonight the fire of God falls and fills our hearts with a burning fire that will send us out all over the country, and across the water to China, Japan, India, and Africa, to tell lost souls the way of salvation!

7. Definitely Endued with Power from on High

The seventh thing that was the secret of why God used D. L. Moody was that he had a very definite enduement with power from on High, a very clear and definite baptism with the Holy Ghost. Moody knew he absolutely had "the baptism with the Holy Ghost"—he had no doubt about it. In his early days he was a great hustler. and had a tremendous desire to do something, but he had no real power. He worked very largely in the energy of the flesh.

But there were two humble Free Methodist women who used to come over to his meetings in the Y.M.C.A. One was "Auntie Cook," and the other, Mrs. Snow. (I think her name was not Snow at that time.) These two women would come to Mr. Moody at the close of his meetings and say, "We are praying for you."

Finally, Mr. Moody became somewhat nettled and said to them one night, "Why are you praying for me? Why don't you pray for the unsaved?"

They replied, "We are praying that you may get the power."

Mr. Moody did not know what that meant, but he got to thinking about it, and then went to these women and said, "I wish you would tell me what you mean." They told him about the definite baptism with the Holy Ghost, and the power that he would receive with it. Then he asked that he might pray with them and not they merely pray for him.

Auntie Cook once told me of the intense fervor with which Mr. Moody prayed on that occasion. She told me in words that I scarcely dare repeat, though I have never forgotten them. And he not only prayed with them, but he also prayed alone.

One day not long after, he was on his way to England and was walking up Wall Street in New York. (Mr. Moody very seldom told this and I almost hesitate to tell it), when in the midst of the bustle and hurry of that city his prayer was answered. The power of God fell upon him as he walked up the street and he had to hurry off to the house of a friend and ask that he might have a room by himself, and in that room he stayed alone for hours. The Holy Ghost came upon him, filling his soul with such joy that at last he had to ask God to withhold His hand, lest he die on the spot from the joy of the Lord. He went out from that place with the power of the Holy Ghost upon him, and when he got to London (partly through the prayers of a bedridden saint in Mr. Lessey's church), the power of God wrought through him mightily in North London, and hundreds were added to the churches. That was what led to his being invited over to the wonderful campaign that followed in later years.

Time and again Mr. Moody would come to me and say, "Torrey, I want you to preach on the baptism with the Holy Ghost." I do not know how many times he asked me to speak on that subject.

At Mr. Moody's suggestion, I had been invited to preach in the Fifth Avenue Presbyterian Church, New York, (had it not been for his suggestion the invitation would never have been extended to me). Just before I started for New York, Mr. Moody drove up to my house and said, "Torrey, they want you to preach at the Fifth Avenue Presbyterian Church in New York. It is a great big church, cost a million dollars to build it." Then he continued, "Torrey, I just want to ask one thing of you. I want to tell you what to preach about. You will preach that sermon of yours on 'Ten Reasons Why I Believe the Bible to Be the Word of God,' and your sermon on 'The Baptism With the Holy Ghost.'"

Time and again, when a call came to me to go off to some church, he would come up to me and say, "Now, Torrey, be sure and preach on the baptism with the Holy Ghost." I do not know how many times he said that to me. Once I asked him, "Mr. Moody, don't you think I have any sermons but those two: 'Ten Reasons Why I Believe the Bible to Be the Word of God' and 'The Baptism With the Holy Ghost'?"

"Never mind that," he replied, "you give them those two sermons."

Once he had some teachers at Northfield—fine men, all of them, but they did not believe in a definite baptism with the Holy Ghost for the individual. They believed that every child of God was baptized with the Holy Ghost, and they did not believe in any special baptism with the Holy Ghost for the individual. Mr. Moody came to me and said: "Torrey, will you come up to my house after the meeting tonight and I will get those men to come, and I want you to talk this thing out with them."

Of course, I very readily consented, and Mr. Moody and I talked for a long time, but they did not altogether see eye to eye with us. And when they went, Mr. Moody signaled me to remain for a few moments. Mr. Moody sat there with his chin on his breast, as he so often sat when he was in deep thought, and then he looked up and said, "Oh, why will they split hairs? Why don't they see that this is just the one thing that they themselves need? They are good teachers, they are wonderful teachers, and I am so glad to have them here, but why will they not see that the baptism with the Holy Ghost is just the one touch that they themselves need?"

I shall never forget the eighth of July, 1894, to my dying day. It was the closing day of the Northfield Students' Conference—the gathering of the students from the eastern colleges. Mr. Moody had asked me to preach on Saturday night and Sunday morning on the baptism with the Holy Ghost. On Saturday night I had spoken about, "The Baptism With the Holy Ghost: What It Is, What It Does, the Need of It, and the Possibility of It." On Sunday morning I spoke on "The Baptism With the Holy Ghost: How to Get It."

It was just exactly twelve o'clock when I finished my morning sermon, and I took out my watch and said, "Mr. Moody has invited us all to go up to the mountain at three o'clock this afternoon to pray for the power of the Holy Ghost. It is three hours to three o'clock. Some of you cannot wait three hours. You do not need to wait. Go to your rooms, go out into the woods, go to your tent, go any place where you can get alone with God and have this matter out with Him."

At three o'clock we all gathered in front of Mr. Moody's mother's house (she was then still living), and then began to pass down the lane, through the gate, up on the mountainside. There were four hundred and fifty-six of us in all—I know the number because Paul Moody counted us as we passed through the gate.

After awhile Mr. Moody said, "I don't think we need to go any farther. Let us sit down here." We sat down on stumps and logs and on the ground. Mr. Moody said, "Have any of you students anything to say?"

I think about seventy-five of them arose, one after the other, and said, "Mr. Moody, I could not wait until three o'clock. I have been alone with God since the morning service, and I believe I have a right to say that I have been baptized with the Holy Ghost."

When these testimonies were over, Mr. Moody said, "Young men, I can't see any reason why we shouldn't kneel down here right now and ask God that the Holy Ghost may fall upon us just as definitely as He fell upon the apostles on the Day of Pentecost. Let us pray."

And we did pray, there on the mountainside. As we had gone up the mountainside heavy clouds had been gathering, and just as we began to pray those clouds broke and the raindrops began to fall through the overhanging pines. But there was another cloud that had been gathering over Northfield for ten days, a cloud big with the mercy and grace and power of God, and as we began to pray our prayers seemed to pierce that cloud and the Holy Ghost fell upon us.

Men and women, that is what we all need, the same thing that D. L. Moody had—the definite baptism with the Holy Ghost.

SECRET POWER
By D. L. Moody

Preface

One man has "zeal without knowledge," while another may have knowledge without zeal. If I could have only the one, I believe I would choose the first. With an open Bible, no one need be without knowledge of God's will and purpose. The object of this book is to help others to know the source of true power; that both their zeal and their knowledge may be of increased service in the Master's work.

Paul says, *"All Scripture is given by inspiration of God, and is profitable for doctrine, reproof, correction and instruction in righteousness; that the man of God may be perfect, thoroughly furnished unto all good works"* (2 Tim. 3:16), but I believe one portion, and that the subject of this book has been too much over looked as though it were not practical, and the result is lack of power in testimony and work. If we would work, "not as one that beats the air," but to some definite purpose, we would have this power from on high. Without this power, our work will be drudgery. With it, it becomes a joyful task, a refreshing service.

May God make this book a blessing to many. This is my prayer.

D. L. Moody
Northfield, Mass., May 1st, 1881

CHAPTER 1

Power: Its Source

*"Without the soul, divinely quickened and inspired,
the observances of the grandest ritualism are as
worthless as the motions of a galvanized corpse."*
Anonymous

I quote this sentence, as it leads me at once to the subject under consideration. What is this quickening and inspiration? What is this power needed? From where is its source? I reply: The Holy Spirit of God. I am a full believer in "The Apostles' Creed," and therefore "I believe in the Holy Ghost." A writer has pointedly asked: "What are our souls without His grace?—as dead as the branch in which the sap does not circulate. What is the Church without Him?—as parched and barren as the fields without the dew and rain of heaven." There has been much inquiry of late on the subject of the Holy Spirit. In this and other lands thousands of persons have been giving attention to the study of this grand theme. I hope it will lead us all to pray for the greater manifestation of His power upon the whole Church of God. How much we have dishonored Him in the past! How ignorant of His grace, and love and presence we have been? True, we have heard of Him and read of Him, but we have had little intelligent knowledge of His attributes, His offices and His relations to us. I fear He has not been to many professed Christians an actual existence, nor do they know him as a personality of the Godhead.

The first work of the Spirit is to give life—spiritual life. He gives it and He sustains it. If there is no life, there can be no power. Solomon says: "A living dog is better than a dead lion" (Eccl. 9:4). When the Spirit imparts this life, He does not leave us to droop and die, but constantly fans the flame. He is ever with us. Surely we ought not to be ignorant of His power and His work.

Identity and Personality

In 1st John 5:7, we read: *"There are three that bear record in heaven, the Father, the Word, and the Holy Ghost, and these three are one."* By the Father is meant the first Person; Christ, the Word is the second; and the Holy Spirit, perfectly fulfilling His own office and work in union with the Father and the Son, is the third. I find clearly presented in my Bible that the One God who demands my love, service and worship, has there revealed Himself, and that each of those three names of the Father, Son and Holy Ghost has personality attached to them. Therefore we find some things ascribed to God as Father, some to God as Savior, and some to God as Comforter and Teacher. It has been remarked that the Father plans, the Son executes, and the Holy Spirit applies. But I also believe they plan and work together. The distinction of persons is often noted in Scripture.

In Matthew 3:16-17, we find Jesus submitting to baptism, the Spirit descending upon Him, while the Father's voice of approval is heard saying: *"This is my Beloved Son in whom I am well pleased."* Again in John 14:16 we read: *"I (i.e. Jesus) will pray the Father, and He shall give you another Comforter."* Also in Ephesians 1:18 *"Through Him (i.e. Christ Jesus) we both (Jews and Gentiles) have access by one Spirit unto the Father."* Thus we are taught the distinction of persons in the Godhead, and their inseparable union. From these and other scriptures also we learn the identity and actual existence of the Holy Spirit.

If you ask do I understand what is thus revealed in Scripture, I say "no." But my faith bows down before the inspired Word and I unhesitatingly believe the great things of God when even reason is blinded and the intellect confused.

In addition to the teaching of God's Word, the Holy Spirit in His gracious work in the soul declares His own presence. Through His agency we are "born again," and through His indwelling we possess superhuman power. Science, falsely so called, when arrayed against the existence and presence of the Spirit of God with His people, only exposes its own folly to the contempt of those who have become "new creatures in Christ Jesus." The Holy Spirit who inspired prophets, and qualified apostles, continues to animate, guide and comfort all true believers. To the actual Christian, the personality of the Holy Spirit is more real than any theory science has to offer, for so-called science is but calculation based on human observation, and is constantly changing its inferences. But the existence of the Holy Spirit is to the child of God a matter of Scripture revelation and of actual experience.

Some skeptics assert that there is no other vital energy in the world but physical force, while contrary to their assertions, thousands and tens of thousands who cannot possibly be deceived have been quickened into spiritual life by a power neither physical or mental. Men who were dead in sins—drunkards who lost their will, blasphemers who lost their purity, libertines sunk in beastliness, infidels who published their shame to the world, have in numberless instances become the subjects of the Spirit's power and are now walking in the true nobility of Christian manhood, separated by an infinite distance from their former life. Let others reject, if they will, at their own peril, this imperishable truth. I believe, and am growing more into this belief, that divine, miraculous creative power resides in the Holy Ghost. Above and beyond all natural law, yet in harmony with it, creation, providence, the Divine government, and the building up of the Church of God are presided over by the Spirit of God.

His ministration is the ministration of life more glorious than the ministration of law, (2 Corinthians 3:16-10). And like the Eternal Son, the Eternal Spirit having life in Himself, is working out all things after the counsel of His own will, and for the everlasting glory of the Triune Godhead.

The Holy Spirit has all the qualities belonging to a person—the power to understand, to will, to do, to call, to feel, to love. This cannot be said of a mere influence. He possesses attributes and qualities, which can only be ascribed to a person, as acts and deeds performed by Him that cannot be performed by a machine, an influence, or a result.

Agent and Instrument

The Holy Spirit is closely identified with the words of the Lord Jesus. *"It is the Spirit that quickens; the flesh profits nothing, the words that I speak unto you, they are spirit and they are life"* (John 6:63). The Gospel proclamation cannot be divorced from the Holy Spirit. Unless He attends the word in power, vain will be the attempt in preaching it. Human eloquence or persuasiveness of speech is the mere trappings of the dead, if the living Spirit is absent. The prophet may preach to the bones in the valley, but it must be the breath from Heaven that will cause the slain to live.

In the third chapter of the First Epistle of Peter, it reads:

> *"For Christ also has once suffered for sins, the just for the unjust, that He might bring us to God, being put to death in the flesh, but quickened by the Spirit"* (1 Peter 3:18).

Here we see that Christ was raised up from the grave by this same "Spirit," and the power exercised to raise Christ's dead body must raise our dead souls and quicken them. No other power on earth can quicken a dead soul, but the same power that raised the body of Jesus Christ out of Joseph's sepulcher. And if we want that power to quicken our friends who are dead in sin, we must look to God, and not be looking to man to do it. If we look alone to ministers; if we look alone to Christ's disciples to do this work, we shall be disappointed. But if we look to the Spirit of God and expect it to come from Him and Him alone, then we shall honor the Spirit, and the Spirit will do His work.

Secret of Efficiency

I cannot help but believe there are many Christians who want to be more efficient in the Lord's service, and the object of this book is to take up this subject of the Holy Spirit, that they may see from whom to expect this power. In the teaching of Christ, we find the last words recorded in the Gospel of Matthew, the 28th chapter and 19th verse, *"Go, therefore, and teach all nations, baptizing them in the name of the Father, and of the Son and of the Holy Ghost."*

Here we find that the Holy Spirit and the Son are equal with the Father—are one with Him, "teaching them in the name of the Father, and of the Son, and of the Holy Ghost." Christ was now handing His commission over to His Apostles. He was going to leave them. His work on earth was finished, and He was now just about ready to take His seat at the right hand of God, and He spoke unto them and said: *"All power is given unto Me in heaven and on earth"* (Matt. 28:18). All power, so then He had authority. If Christ was mere man, as some people try to make out, it would have been blasphemy for Him to have said to the disciples, go and baptize all nations in the name of the Father, and in His own name, and in that of the Holy Ghost, making Himself equal with the Father.

There are three things: All Power is given unto Me; go teach all nations.

Teach them what? To observe all things. There are a great many people now that are willing to observe what they like about Christ, but the things that they don't like they just dismiss and turn away from. But His commission to His disciples was, "Go teach all nations to observe all things whatsoever I have commanded you." And what right has a messenger who has been sent of God to change the message? If I had sent a servant to deliver a message, and the servant thought the message didn't sound exactly right—a little harsh—and that servant went and changed the message, I should change servants very quickly; he could not serve me any longer. And when a minister or a messenger of Christ begins to change the message, because he thinks it is not exactly what it ought to be and thinks that he is wiser than God, God just dismisses that man.

They haven't taught "all things." They have left out some of the things that Christ has commanded us to teach, because they didn't correspond with man's reason. Now we have to take the Word of God just as it is; and if we are going to take it, we have no authority to take out just what we like, what we think is appropriate, and let dark reason be our guide.

It is the work of the Spirit to impress the heart and seal the preached word. His office is to take of the things of Christ and reveal them unto us.

Some people have an idea that this is the only dispensation of the Holy Ghost; that He didn't work until Christ was glorified. But Simeon felt the Holy Ghost when he went into the temple in 2 Peter 1:21, we read: *"Holy men of old spoke as they were moved by the Holy Ghost."* We find the same Spirit in Genesis as is seen in Revelation. The same Spirit that guided the hand that wrote Exodus inspired also the epistles, and we find the same Spirit speaking from one end of the Bible to the other. So holy men in all ages have spoken as they were moved by the Holy Spirit.

His Personality

I was a Christian a long time before I found out that the Holy Ghost was a person. Now this is something a great many don't seem to understand, but if you will just take up the Bible and see what Christ had to say about the Holy Spirit, you would find that He always spoke of Him as a person—never spoke of Him as an influence. Some people have an idea that the Holy Spirit is an attribute of God, just like mercy—just an influence coming from God. But we find in the fourteenth chapter of John, sixteenth verse, these words:

"And I will pray the Father, and He shall give you another Comforter that He may abide with you forever." And again, in the same chapter, seventeenth verse: "Even the Spirit of Truth, whom the world cannot receive, because it sees Him not, neither knows Him; but you know Him; for He dwells with you and shall be in you."

Again, in the twenty-sixth verse of the same chapter:

"But the Comforter, which is the Holy Ghost, whom the Father will send in my name He shall teach you all things, and bring all things to your remembrance whatsoever I have said unto you."

Observe the pronouns "He" and "Him." I want to call attention to this fact that whenever Christ spoke of the Holy Ghost He spoke of Him as a person, not a mere influence. If we want to honor the Holy Ghost, let us bear in mind that He is one of the Trinity, a person of the Godhead.

The Reservoir of Love

We read that the fruit of the Spirit is love. God is love, Christ is love, and we should not be surprised to read about the love of the Spirit. What a blessed attribute is this. May I call it the dome of the temple of the graces.

Better still, it is the crown of crowns worn by the Triune God. Human love is a natural emotion that flows forth towards the object of our affections. But Divine love is as high above human love as the heaven is above the earth. The natural man is of the earth, earthy, and however pure his love may be, it is weak and imperfect at best. But the love of God is perfect and entire, wanting nothing. It is as mighty ocean in its greatness, dwelling with and flowing from the Eternal Spirit.

In Romans 5:5, we read: *"And hope makes not ashamed, because the love of God is shed abroad in our hearts by the Holy Ghost which is given to us."* Now if we are co-workers with God, there is one thing we must possess, and that is love. A man may be a very successful lawyer and have no love for his clients, and yet get on very well. A man may be a very successful physician and have no love for his patients, and yet be a very good physician. A man may be a very successful merchant and have no love for his customers, and yet he may do a good business and succeed. But no man can be a co-worker with God without love. If our service is mere profession on our part, the quicker we renounce it the better. If a man takes up God's work as he would take up any profession, the sooner he gets out of it the better.

We cannot work for God without love. It is the only tree that can produce fruit on this sin-cursed earth, which is acceptable to God. If I have no love for God or for my fellow man, then I cannot work acceptably. I am like sounding brass and a tinkling cymbal. We are told that the *"love of God is shed abroad in our hearts by the Holy Ghost."* (Rom. 5:5). Now, if we have had that love shed abroad in our hearts, we are ready for God's service; if we have not, we are not ready. It is so easy to reach a man when you love him, all barriers are broken down and swept away.

Paul when writing to Titus, second chapter and first verse, tells him to be sound in faith, in charity, and in patience. Now in this age, ever since I can remember, the Church has been very jealous about men being unsound in the faith. If a man becomes unsound in the faith, they draw their ecclesiastical sword and cut at him; but he may be ever so unsound in love, and they don't say anything. He may be ever so defective in patience; he may be irritable and fretful all the time, but they never deal with him.

Now the Bible teaches us, that we are not only to be sound in the faith, but in charity and in patience. I believe God cannot use many of His servants, because they are full of irritability and impatience; they are fretting all the time, from morning until night. God cannot use them, for their mouths are sealed and they cannot speak for Jesus Christ. If they have not love, they cannot work for God. I do not mean love for those that love me; it doesn't take grace to do that. The rudest savage in the world can do that; the vilest man that every walked the earth can do that. It doesn't take any grace at all. I did that before I ever became a Christian. Love begets love and hatred begets hatred.

If I know a man loves me first, I know my love will be going out towards him. Suppose a man comes to me, saying, "Mr. Moody, a certain man told me today that he thought you were the meanest man living." Well, if I didn't have a good deal of the grace of God in my heart, then I know there would be hard feelings that would spring up in my heart against that man, and it would not be long before I would be talking against him. Hatred begets hatred.

But suppose a man comes to me and says, "Mr. Moody, do you know that such a man that I met today says that he thinks a great deal of you?" Though I may never have heard of him, there would be love springing up in my heart. Love begets love; we all know that; but it takes the grace of God to love the man that lies about me, the man that slanders me, the man that is trying to tear down my character. It takes the grace of God to love that man. You may hate the sin he has committed, yet there is a difference between the sin and the sinner. You may hate the one with a perfect hatred, but you must love the sinner. I cannot otherwise do him any good. Now you know the first impulse of a young convert is to love. Do you remember the day you were converted? Was not your heart full of sweet peace and love?

The Right Overflow

I remember the morning I came out of my room after I had first trusted Christ, and I thought the old sun shone a good deal brighter than it ever had before. I thought that the sun was just smiling upon me, and I walked out upon Boston Common, and I heard the birds in the trees, and I thought that they were all singing a song for me. Do you know I fell in love with the birds? I never cared for them before; it seemed to me that I was in love with all creation. I had not a bitter feeling against any man, and I was ready to

93

take all men to my heart. If a man has not the love of God shed abroad in his heart, he has never been regenerated. If you hear a person get up in a prayer meeting, and he begins to speak and find fault with everybody, you may know that his is not a genuine conversion; it is counterfeit. It has not the right ring, because the impulse of a converted soul is to love, and not to be getting up and complaining of every one else, and finding fault.

But it is hard for us to live in the right atmosphere all the time. Someone comes along and treats us wrongly, perhaps we hate him. We have not attended to the means of grace and kept feeding on the word of God as we ought; a root of bitterness springs up in our hearts, and perhaps we are not aware of it, but it has come up in our hearts; then we are not qualified to work for God. The love of God is not shed abroad in our hearts as it ought to be by the Holy Ghost.

But the work of the Holy Ghost is to impart love. Paul could say, *"The Love of Christ constrains me"* (2 Cor. 5:14). He could not help going from town to town and preaching the Gospel. Jeremiah at one time said: *"I will speak no more in the Lord's name; I have suffered enough; these people don't like God's Word."* They lived in a wicked day, as we do now. Infidels were creeping up all around him, who said the word of God was not true; Jeremiah stood like a wall of fire, confronting them, and he boldly proclaimed that the Word of God was true. At last they put him in prison, and he said: "I will keep still; it has cost me too much." But a little while after, you know, he could not keep still. His bones caught fire; he had to speak. And when we are so full of the Love of God, we are compelled to work for God, then God blesses us. If our work accomplished by the lash, without any true motive power, it will come to nought.

Now the question comes up, have we the love of God shed abroad in our hearts and are we holding the truth in love? Some people hold the truth, but in such a cold stern way that it will do no good. Other people want to love everything, and so they give up much of the truth; but we are to hold the truth in love; we are to hold the truth even if we lose all, but we are to hold it in love, and if we do that, the Lord will bless us.

There are a good many people trying to get this love; and they are trying to produce it of themselves. But therein all fail. The love implanted deep in our new nature will be spontaneous. I don't have to learn to love my children. I cannot help loving them. Some time ago during an inquiry meeting a young miss said that she could not love God; that it was very hard for her to love Him. I said to her, "Is it hard for you to love your Mother? Do you have to learn to love your Mother?" And she looked up through her tears, and said, "No; I can't help it; that is spontaneous." "Well," I said, "when the Holy Spirit kindles love in your heart, you cannot help loving God; it will be spontaneous." When the Spirit of God comes into your heart and mine, it will be easy to serve God.

The fruit of the Spirit, as you find it in Galatians, begins with love. There are nine graces spoken of in the sixth chapter, and of the nine different graces, Paul puts love at the head of the list; love is the first thing—the first in that precious cluster of fruit. Someone has put it in this way: that all the other eight can be put in the word "love." Joy is love exulting; peace is love in repose; long-suffering is love on trial; gentleness is love in society; goodness is love in action; faith is love on the battlefield; meekness is love at school; and temperance is love in training. So it is love all the way; love at the top; love at the bottom, and all the way along down these graces. If we only just brought forth the fruit of the Spirit, what a world we would have. There would be no need of any policemen. A man could leave his overcoat around without some one stealing it, and men would not have any desire to do evil. Says Paul, "Against such there is no law," you don't need any law. A man who is full of the Spirit doesn't need to be put under law; doesn't need any policemen to watch him. We could dismiss all our policemen; the lawyers would have to give up practicing law, and the courts would not have any business.

The Triumphs of Hope

In the fifteenth chapter of Romans, thirteenth verse, the Apostle says: *"Now the God of hope fill you with all joy and peace in believing, that you may abound in hope through the power of the Holy Ghost."* The next thing then is hope.

Did you ever notice this, that no man or woman is ever used by God to build up His kingdom who has lost hope? Now, I have been observing this throughout different parts of the country, and wherever I have found a worker in God's vineyard who has lost hope, I have found a man or woman not very useful. Now, just look at these workers. Let your mind go over the past for a moment. Can you think of a man or woman whom God has used to build His kingdom that has lost hope? I don't know of any; I never heard of such a one. It is very important to have hope in the Church, and it is the work of the Holy Ghost to impart hope. Let Him come into some of the churches where there have not been any conversions for a few years, and let Him convert a score of people, and see how hopeful the Church becomes at once. He imparts hope; a man filled with the Spirit of God will be very hopeful. He will be looking out into the future, and he knows that it is all-bright, because the God of all grace is able to do great things. So it is very important that we have hope.

If a man has lost hope, he is out of communion with God, he has not the Spirit of God resting upon him for service. He may be a son of God, but disheartened so that he cannot be used of God. Do you know there is no place in the Scriptures where it is recorded that God ever used even a discouraged man.

Some years ago, in my work I was quite discouraged, and I was ready to hang my harp on the willow. I was very much cast down and depressed. I had been for weeks in that state, when one Monday morning a friend, who had a very large Bible class, came into my study. I used to examine the notes of his Sunday School lessons, which were equal to a sermon, and he came to me this morning and said, "Well, what did you preach about yesterday?" and I told him.

Then I said, "What did you preach about?" and he said that he preached about Noah. "Did you ever preach about Noah?" "No, I never preached about Noah." "Did you ever study his character?" "No, I never studied his life particularly." "Well," he said, "he is a most wonderful character. It will do you good. You ought to study up that character."

When he went out, I took down my Bible, and read about Noah; and then it came over me that Noah worked 120 years and never had a convert, and yet he did not get discouraged. I said, "Well, I ought not to be discouraged," and I closed my Bible, got up and walked down town, and the cloud had gone. I went down to the noon prayer meeting, and heard of a little town in the country where they had taken into the church 100 young converts; and I said to myself, I wonder what Noah would have given if he could have heard that; and yet he worked 120 years and didn't get discouraged. And then a man right across the aisle got up and said, "My friends, I wish for you to pray for me; I think I'm lost;" and I thought to myself, "I wonder what Noah would have given to hear that." He never heard a man say, "I wish for you to pray for me; I think I am lost," and yet he didn't get discouraged!

Oh, children of God, let us not get discouraged. Let us ask God to forgive us, if we have been discouraged and cast down. Let us ask God to give us hope, that we may be ever hopeful. It does me good sometimes to meet some people and take hold of their hands; they are so hopeful, while other people throw a gloom over me because they are all the time cast down, and looking at the dark side, and looking at the obstacles and difficulties that are in the way.

The Blessing of Liberty

The next thing the Spirit of God does is to give us liberty. He first imparts love; He next inspires hope, and then gives liberty, and that is about the last thing we have in a good many of our churches at the present day. And I am sorry to say there must be a funeral in a good many churches before there is much work done. We would have to bury the formalism so deep that it will never have any resurrection. The last thing to be found in many a church is liberty.

If the Gospel happens to be preached, the people criticize, as they would a theatrical performance. It is exactly the same, and many a professed Christian never thinks of listening to what the man of God has to say. It is hard work to preach to carnally minded critics, but "Where the Spirit of the Lord is, there is liberty." Very often a woman will hear a hundred goods things in a sermon, and there may be one thing that strikes her as a little out of place, and she will go home and sit down to the table and talk right out before her children and magnify that one wrong thing, and not say a word about the hundred good things that were said. That is what people do who criticize.

God does not use men in captivity. The condition of many is like Lazarus when he came out of the sepulcher bound hand and foot. The bandage was not taken off his mouth, and he could not speak. He had life, and if you had said Lazarus was not alive, you would have told a falsehood, because he was raised from the dead. There are a great many people, the moment you talk to them and insinuate they are not doing what they might, they say: "I have life. I am a Christian." Well, you can't deny it, but they are bound hand and foot.

May God snap these fetters and set His children free, that they may have liberty. I believe He comes to set us free, and wants us to work for Him, and speak for Him. How many people would like to get up in a social prayer meeting to say a few words for Christ, but there is such a cold spirit of criticism in the Church that they dare not do it. They have not the liberty to do it. If they get up, there are so frightened with these critics that they begin to tremble and sit down. They cannot say anything. Now, that is all wrong. The Spirit of God comes just to give liberty, and wherever you see the Lord's work going on, you will see that Spirit of liberty. People won't be afraid of speaking to one another. And when the meeting is over they will not get their hats and see how quick they can get out of the church, but will begin to shake hands with one another, and there will be liberty there. A good many go to the prayer meeting out of a mere cold sense of duty. They think "I must attend because I feel it is my duty." They don't think it is a glorious privilege to meet and pray, and to be strengthened, and to help some one else in the wilderness journey.

What we need today is love in our hearts. Don't we want it? Don't we want hope in our lives? Don't we want to be hopeful? Don't we want liberty? Now, all this is the work of the Spirit of God, and let us pray to God daily to give us love, and hope, and liberty. We read in Hebrews, *"Having, therefore, brethren, boldness to enter into the holiest by the blood of Jesus."* If you will turn to the passage and read the margin, it says: *"Having, therefore, brethren, liberty to enter into the holiest."* We can go into the holiest, having freedom of access, and plead for this love and liberty and glorious hope, that we may not rest until God gives us power to work for Him.

If I know my own heart today, I would rather die than live as I once did, a mere nominal Christian, and not used by God in building up His kingdom.

It seems a poor empty life to live for the sake of self.

Let us seek to be useful. Let us seek to be vessels meet for the Master's use that God, the Holy Spirit, may shine fully through us.

CHAPTER 2

Power: "In" and "Upon"

The Holy Spirit dwelling in us, is one thing; I think this is clearly brought out in Scripture; and the Holy Spirit upon us for service, is another thing.

Now there are only three places we find in Scripture that are dwelling places for the Holy Ghost.

In the 40th chapter of Exodus, commencing with the 33rd verse, are these words:

"And he (that is Moses) reared up the court round about the tabernacle and the altar, and set up the hanging of the court gate. So Moses finished the work."

"Then a cloud covered the tent of the congregation, and the glory of the Lord filled the tabernacle" *(Exod. 40:34).*

"And Moses was not able to enter into the tent of the congregation, because the cloud abode thereon, and the glory of the Lord filled the tabernacle" *(Exod. 40:35).*

The moment that Moses finished the work, the moment that the tabernacle was ready, the cloud came, the Shekinah glory came and filled it so that Moses was not able to stand before the presence of the Lord. I believe firmly, that the moment our hearts are emptied of pride and selfishness and ambition and self-seeking, and everything that is contrary to God's law, the Holy Ghost will come and fill every corner of our hearts; but if we are full of pride and conceit, and ambition and self-seeking, and pleasure and the world, there is no room for the Spirit of God. I believe many a man is praying to God to fill him when he is full already with something else. Before we pray that God would fill us, I believe we ought to pray Him to empty us.

There must be an emptying before there can be a filling; and when the heart is turned upside down, and everything is turned out that is contrary to God, then the Spirit will come, just as He did in the tabernacle, and fill us with His Glory. We read in 2nd Chronicles, 5th chapter and 13th verse:

> "It came even to pass, as the trumpeters and singers were as one to make one sound, to be heard in praising and thanking the Lord, and when they lifted up their voice with the trumpets and cymbals and instruments of music, and praised the Lord, saying, For He is good; for His mercy endures forever; that then the house was filled with a cloud, even the house of the Lord. So that the priests could not stand to minister by reason of the cloud, for the glory of the Lord had filled the house of God."

Praising With One Heart

We find, the very moment that Solomon completed the Temple, when all was finished, they were just praising God with one hear—the choristers and the singers and the ministers were all one; there was not any discord; they were all praising God, and the glory of God came and just filled the Temple as the Tabernacle. Now, as you turn over into the New Testament, you will find, instead of coming to Tabernacles and Temples, believers are now the Temple of the Holy Ghost. When on the day of Pentecost, before Peter preached that memorable sermon, as they were praying, the Holy Ghost came, and came in mighty power. We now pray for the Spirit of God to come and we sing:

Come, Holy Spirit, heavenly dove,
With all thy quickening power;
Kindle a flame of heavenly love
In these cold hearts of ours.

I believe, if we understand it, it is perfectly right; but if we are praying for Him to come out of heaven down to earth again, that is wrong, because He is already here! He has not been out of this earth 1800 years. He has been in the Church, and He is with all believers. The believers in the Church are the called-out ones, they are called out from the world, and every true believer is a Temple for the Holy Ghost to dwell in. In the 14th chapter of John, 17th verse, we have the words of Jesus:

"The Spirit of Truth, whom the world cannot receive, because it sees Him not, neither knows Him; but you know Him, for He dwells in you."

"*Greater is He that is in you than He that is in the World.*" If we have the Spirit dwelling in us, He gives us power over the flesh and the world, and over every enemy. "*He is dwelling with you, and shall be in you.*" Read 1st Corinthians 3:16: "*Do you not know that you are the temple of God, and that the Spirit of God dwells in you?*"

There were some men burying an aged saint some time ago, and he was very poor, like many of God's people, poor in this world, but they are very rich, they have all the riches on the other side of life—they have them laid up there where thieves cannot get them, and where moth cannot corrupt—so this aged man was very rich in the other world, and they were just hastening him off to the grave, wanting to get rid of him, when and old minister who was officiating at the grave, said, "Tread softly, for you are carrying the temple of the Holy Ghost." Whenever you see a believer, you see a temple of the Holy Ghost.

In 1 Corinthians 6:19-20, we read again:

"*Do you not know that your body is the temple of the Holy Ghost which is in you, which you have of God, and you are not your own for you are bought with a price, therefore glorify God in your body and in your spirit, which are God's.*"

Thus are we taught that there is a divine resident in every child of God.

I think it is clearly taught in the Scripture that every believer has the Holy Ghost dwelling in him. He may be quenching the Spirit of God, and he may not glorify God as he should, but if he is a believer in the Lord Jesus

Christ, the Holy Ghost dwells in him. But I want to call your attention to another fact. I believe today, that though Christian men and women have the Holy Spirit dwelling in them, yet He is not dwelling within them in power; in other words, God has a great many sons and daughters without power.

1. What is Needed

Nine-tenths, at least, of the church members never think of speaking for Christ. If they see a man, perhaps a near relative, just going right down to ruin, going rapidly, they never think of speaking to him about his sinful course and of seeking to win him to Christ. Now certainly there must be something wrong. And yet when you talk with them you find they have faith, and you cannot say they are not children of God. But they have not the power, they have not the liberty, they have not the love that real disciples of Christ should have.

A great many people are thinking that we need new measures, that we need new churches, that we need new organs, and that we need new choirs, and all these new things. That is not what the Church of God needs today. It is the old power that the Apostles had; that is what we want, and if we have that in our churches, there will be new life. Then we will have new ministers—the same old ministers renewed with power and filled with the Spirit.

I remember when in Chicago many were toiling in the work, and it seemed as though the car of salvation didn't move on, when a minister began to cry out from the very depths of his heart, "Oh, God, put new ministers in every pulpit." On next Monday I heard two or three men stand up and say, "We had a new minister last Sunday—the same old minister, but he received new power." I firmly believe that is what we want today all over America. We want new ministers in the pulpit and new people in the pews. We want people quickened by the Spirit of God, and the Spirit coming down and taking possession of the children of God and giving them power.

Then a man filled with the Spirit will know how to use "the sword of the Spirit." If a man is not filled with the Spirit, he will never know how to use the Book. We are told that this is the sword of the Spirit, and what is an army good for that does not know how to uses its weapons? Suppose a battle is going on, and I were a general and had a hundred thousand men, great, able-bodied men, full of life, but they could not one of them handle a sword, and not one of them knew how to use his rifle, what would that army be good for? Why, one thousand well-drilled men, with good weapons, would rout the whole of them. The reason why the Church cannot overcome the enemy is, because she doesn't know how to use the sword of the Spirit. People will get up and try to fight the devil with their experiences, but he doesn't care for that, he will overcome them every time. People are trying to fight the devil with theories and pet ideas, but he will get the victory over them likewise. What we want is to draw the sword of the Spirit. It is that which cuts deeper than anything else.

Turn in your Bibles to Ephesians 6:14:

"Stand, therefore, having your loins girded about with truth, and having on the breastplate of righteousness; and your feet shod with the preparation of the gospel of peace; above all (or over all), taking the shield of faith, wherewith you

shall be able to quench all the fiery darts of the wicked. And take the helmet of salvation and the sword of the Spirit, which is the Word of God."

The Greatest Weapon

The sword of the Spirit is the Word of God, and what we need specially is to be filled with the Spirit, so we shall know how to use the Word. There was a Christian man talking to a skeptic, who was using the Word, and the skeptic said, "I don't believe, sir, in that Book." But the man went right on, and he gave him more of the Word, and the man again remarked, "I don't believe the Word," but he kept giving him more, and at last the man was reached. And the brother added, "When I have proved a good sword which does the work of execution, I would just keep right on using it."

That is what we want. Skeptics and infidels may say they don't believe in it. It is not our work to make them believe in it; that is the work of the Spirit. Our work is to give them the Word of God; not to preach our theories and our ideas about it, but just to deliver the message as God gives it to us.

We read in the Scriptures of the Sword of the Lord and Gideon. Suppose Gideon had gone out without the Word, he would have been defeated. But the Lord used Gideon, and I think you find all through the Scriptures that God takes up and uses human instruments. You cannot find, I believe, a case in the Bible where a man is converted without God calling in some human agency—using some human instrument; not that He can't do it in His independent sovereignty; there is no doubt about that. Even when by the revealed glory of the Lord Jesus, Saul of Tarsus was smitten to the earth, Annanias was used to open his eyes and lead him into the light of the Gospel.

I heard a man once say, if you put a man on a mountain peak that is higher than one of the Alpine peaks, God could save him without a human messenger; but that is not His way; that is not His method; but it is "The sword of the Lord and Gideon;" and the Lord and Gideon will do the work. If we are just willing to let the Lord use us, He will.

"None of Self"

Then you will find all through the Scriptures, when men were filled with the Holy Spirit, they preached Christ and not themselves. They preached Christ and Him crucified. It says in the first chapter of Luke, 67th Verse, speaking of Zacharias, the father of John the Baptist:

> "And his father, Zacharias, was filled with the Holy Ghost, and prophesied, saying: Blessed be the Lord God of Israel, for He has visited and redeemed His people, and has raised up a horn of salvation for us in the house of His servant David. As He spoke by the mouth of His Holy prophets, which have been since the world began."

See, he is talking about the Word. If a man is filled with the Spirit, he will magnify the Word; he will preach the Word, and not himself; he will give this lost world the Word of the living God.

"And you, child, shall be called the prophet of the Highest; for you shall go before the face of the Lord to prepare His ways. To give knowledge of salvation unto His people by the remission of their sins, through the tender mercy of our God, whereby the day-spring from on high has visited us. To give light to them that sit in darkness and in the shadow of death, to guide our feet into the way of peace. And the child grew and waxed strong in spirit, and was in the deserts till the day of his showing unto Israel" (Luke 1:76-80).

And so we find again that when Elizabeth and Mary met, they talked of the Scriptures, and they were both filled with the Holy Ghost, and at once began to talk of their Lord.

We also find that Simeon, as he came into the temple and found the young child Jesus there, at once began to quote the Scriptures, for the Spirit was upon him. And when Peter stood up on the day of Pentecost, and preached that wonderful sermon, it is said he was filled with the Holy Ghost, and began to preach the Word to the multitude, and it was the Word that cut them. It was the sword of the Lord and Peter, the same as it was the sword of the Lord and Gideon. And we find it says of Stephen, *"They were not able to resist the spirit and wisdom by which he spoke."* Why? Because he gave them the Word of God. And we are told that the Holy Ghost came on Stephen, and none could resist his word. And we read, too, that Paul was full of the Holy Spirit, and that he preached Christ and Him crucified, and that many people were added to the Church.

Barnabas was full of faith and the Holy Ghost; and if you will just read and find out what he preached, you

109

will find it was the Word, and many were added to the Lord. So that when a man is full of the Spirit, he begins to preach, not himself, but Christ, as revealed in the Holy Scriptures.

The disciples of Jesus were all filled with the Spirit, and the Word was published. When the Spirit of God comes down upon the Church, and we are anointed the Word will be published in the streets, and in the lanes, and in the alleys. There will not be a dark cellar nor a dark attic, nor a home where the Gospel will not be carried by some loving heart, if the Spirit comes upon God's people in demonstration and in power.

Spiritual Irrigation

It is possible a man may just barely have life and be satisfied, and I think that a great many are in that condition. In the 3rd chapter of John we find that Nicodemus came to Christ and that he received life. At first this life was feeble. You don't hear of him standing up confessing Christ boldly, and of the Spirit coming upon him in great power, though possessing life through faith in Christ. And then in the 4th chapter of John you will find it speaks of the woman coming to the well of Samaria, and Christ held out the cup of salvation to her and she took it and drank, and it became in her *"a well of water springing up into everlasting life."* That is better than in the 3rd chapter of John; here it came down in a flood into her soul; as someone has said, it came down from the throne of God, and like a mighty current carried her back to the throne of God.

Water always rises to its level, and if we get the soul filled with water from the throne of God it will bear us upward to its source. But if you want to get the best class of Christian life portrayed, turn to the 7th chapter and you will find that it says he that receives the Spirit, through trusting in the Lord Jesus, *"Out of him shall flow rivers of living water."* Now there are two ways of digging a well. I remember, when a boy, upon a farm, in New England, they had a well, and they put in an old wooden pump, and I used to have to pump the water from that well upon wash-day, and to water the cattle; and I had to pump and pump and pump until my arm got tired, many a time. But they have a better way now; they don't dig down a few feet and brick up the hole and put the pump in, but they go down through the clay and the sand and the rock, and on down until they strike what they call a lower stream, and then it becomes an artesian well, which needs no labor, as the water rises spontaneously from the depths beneath.

Now I think God wants all His children to be a sort of artesian well; not to keep pumping, but to flow right out. Why, haven't you seen ministers in the pulpit just pumping, and pumping and pumping? I have, many a time, and I have had to do it, too. I know how it is. They stand in the pulpit and talk and talk and talk, and the people go to sleep, they can't arouse them.

What is the trouble? Why, the living water is not there; they are just pumping when there is no water in the well. You can't get water out of a dry well; you have to get something in the well, or you can't get anything out. I have seen these wooden pumps where you have to pour water into them before you could pump any water out, and so it is with a good many people; you have to get something in them before you can get anything out. People wonder why it is that they have no Spiritual power. They stand up and talk in a meeting and don't say anything; they say they

111

haven't anything to say, and you find it out soon enough; they need not state it; but they just talk, because they feel it is a duty, and say nothing.

Now I tell you when the Spirit of God is on us for service, resting upon us, we are anointed, and then we can do great things. *"I will pour water on him that is thirsty,"* says God. O blessed thought—*"He that hungers and thirsts after righteousness shall be filled!"*

Overflowing Streams

I would like to see someone just full of living water; so full that they couldn't contain it; that they would have to go out and publish the Gospel of the grace of God. When a man gets so full that he can't hold any more, then he is just ready for God's service.

When preaching in Chicago, Dr. Gibson remarked in the inquiry meeting, "Now, how can we find out who is thirsty?" He said, "I was just thinking how we could find out. If a boy should come down the aisle, bringing a good pail full of clear water, and a dipper, we would soon find out who was thirsty; we would see thirsty men and women reach out for water; but if you should walk down the aisle with an empty bucket, you wouldn't find it out. People would look in and see that there was no water, and say nothing." So he said, "I think that is the reason we are not more blessed in our ministry; we are carrying around empty buckets, and the people see that we have not anything in them, and they don't come forward." I think that there is a good deal of truth in that. People see that we are carrying around empty buckets, and they will not come to us until they are filled.

They see we haven't any more than they have. We must have the Spirit of God resting upon us, and then we will have something that gives the victory over the world, the flesh, and the devil; something that gives the victory over our tempers, over our conceits, and over every other evil, and when we can trample these sins under our feet, then people will come to us and say, "How did you get it? I need this power; you have something that I haven't got and I want it." O, may God show us this truth. Have we been toiling all night? Let us throw the net on the right side. Let us ask God to forgive our sins and anoint us with power from on high. But remember, He is not going to give this power to an impatient man; He is not going to give to a selfish man; He will never give it to an ambitious man whose aim is selfish, till first emptied of self—emptied of pride and of all worldly thoughts. Let it be God's glory and not our own that we seek and when we get to that point, how speedily the Lord will bless us for good. Then will the measure of our blessing be full. Do you know what heaven's measure is? Good measure, pressed down, shaken together, and running over. If we get out heart filled with the Word of God, how is Satan going to get in? How is the world going to get in, for heaven's measure is good measure, full measure, running over. Have you this fullness? If you have not, then seek it! Say by the grace of God you will have it, for it is the Father's good pleasure to give us these things. He wants us to shine down in this world. He wants to lift us up for His work. He wants us to have the power to testify for His Son. He has left us in this world to testify for Him. What did He leave us for? Not to buy and sell and to get gain, but to glorify Christ. How are you going to do it without the Spirit? That is the question. How are you to do it without the power of God?

Why Some Fail

We read in John 20:22: *"And when He had said this, He breathed on them, and said to them, Receive the Holy Ghost."*

Then see Luke 24:49: *"And behold, I send the promise of my Father upon you; but tarry in the city of Jerusalem until you are endued with power from on high."*

The first passage tells us He had raised those pierced and wounded hands over them and breathed upon them and said, *"Receive the Holy Ghost."* And I haven't a doubt they received it then, but not in such mighty power as afterward when qualified for their work. It was not in fullness that He gave it to them then, but if they had been like a good many now, they would have said, "I have enough now; I am not going to tarry; I am going to work."

Some people seem to think they are losing time if they wait on God for His power and so away they go and work without unction. They are working without any anointing, they are working without any power. But after Jesus had said "Receive the Holy Ghost," and had breathed on them, He said: "Now you tarry in Jerusalem until you be endued with power from on high." Read in the 1st chapter of Acts, 8th verse: *"But you shall receive power, after that the Holy Ghost is come upon you."*

Now, the Spirit had been given them certainly or they could not have believed, and they could not have taken their stand for God and gone through what they did, and endured the scoffs and frowns of their friends, if they had not been converted by the power of the Holy Ghost. But now see what Christ said:

"You shall receive power after that the Holy Ghost is come upon you; and you shall be witnesses unto me both in Jerusalem and in all Judea, and in Samaria, and unto the uttermost pasts of the earth."

Then the Holy Spirit *in* us is one thing, and the Holy Spirit *on* us is another; and if these Christians had gone out and went right to preaching then and there, without the power, do you think that scene would have taken place on the day of Pentecost? Don't you think that Peter would have stood up there and beat against the air, while these Jews would have gnashed their teeth and mocked him? But they tarried in Jerusalem; they waited ten days. What, you say! What, the world perishing and men dying! Shall I wait? Do what God tells you.

There is no use in running before you are sent. There is no use in attempting to do God's work without God's power. A man working without this unction, a man working without this anointing, a man working without the Holy Ghost upon him, is losing his time after all. So we are not going to lose anything if we tarry till we get this power. That is the object of true service, to wait on God, to tarry till we receive this power for witness-bearing.

Then we find that on the day of Pentecost, ten days after Jesus Christ was glorified, the Holy Spirit descended in power. Do you think that Peter and James and John and those apostles doubted it from that very hour? They never doubted it. Perhaps some question the possibility of having the power of God now, and that the Holy Spirit never came afterward in similar manifestation, and will never come again in such power.

Fresh Supplies

In Acts 4:31, you will find He came a second time, and at a place where they were, so that the earth was shaken, and they were filled with this power. That is, we are leaky vessels, and we have to keep right under the fountain all the time to keep full of Christ, and so have a fresh supply.

I believe this is a mistake a great many of us are making. We are trying to do God's work with the grace God gave us ten years ago. We say, if it is necessary, we will go on with the same grace. Now, what we want is a fresh supply, a fresh anointing and fresh power, and if we seek it, and seek it with all our hearts, we will obtain it. The early converts were taught to look for that power. Philip went to Samaria, and news reached Jerusalem that there was a great work being done in Samaria, and many converts; and John and Peter went down, and they laid their hand on them and they received the Holy Ghost for service. I think that is what we Christians ought to be looking for—the Spirit of God for service—that God may use us mightily in the building of His Church and hastening His glory.

In Acts 19 we read of twelve men at Ephesus, who, when the inquiry was made if they had received the Holy Ghost since they believe, answered: *"We have not so much as heard whether there be any Holy Ghost."* I venture to say there are very many, who, if you were to ask them, "Have you received the Holy Ghost since you believed?" would reply, "I don't know what you mean by that." They would be like the twelve men down at Ephesus, who had never understood the peculiar relation of the Spirit to the sons of God in this dispensation. I firmly believe that the Church has just laid this knowledge aside, mislaid it somewhere, and so Christians are without power. Sometimes you can take one hundred members into the Church, and they don't add to its power. Now that is all wrong. If they were only anointed by the Spirit of God, there would be great power if one hundred saved ones were added to the Church.

Green Fields

When I was out in California, the first time I went down from the Sierra Nevada Mountains and dropped into the Valley of the Sacramento, I was surprised to find on one farm that everything about it was green—all the trees and flowers, everything was blooming, and everything was green and beautiful, and just across the hedge everything was dried up, and there was not a green thing there, and I could not understand it. I made inquiries, and I found that the man that had everything green, irrigated; he just poured the water right on, and he kept everything green, while the fields that were next to his were as dry as Gideon's fleece without a drop of dew; and so it is with a great many in the Church today. They are like these farms in California—a dreary desert, everything parched and desolate, and apparently no life in them. They can sit next to a man who is full of the Spirit of God, who is like a green bay tree, and who is bringing forth fruit, and yet they will not seek a similar blessing. Well, why this difference? Because God has poured water on him that was thirsty. That is the difference. One has been seeking this anointing, and he has received it. When we want this above everything else God will surely give it to us.

The great question before us now is, do we want it? I remember when I first went to England and gave a Bible reading, I think about the first that I gave in that country, a great many ministers were there, and I didn't know anything about English theology, and I was afraid I should run against their creeds, and I was a little hampered, especially on this very subject, about the gift of the Holy Spirit for service. I remember particularly a Christian minister there who had his head bowed on his hand, and I thought the good man was ashamed of everything I was saying, and of course that troubled me.

At the close of my address he took his hat and away he went, and then I thought, "Well, I shall never see him again." At the next meeting I looked all around for him, and he wasn't there, and at the next meeting I looked again, but he was absent; and I thought my teaching must have given him offense.

But a few days after that, at a large noon prayer meeting, a man stood up and his face shone as if he had been up in the mountain with God, and I looked at him, and to my great joy it was this brother. He said he was at the Bible reading, and he heard there was such a thing as having fresh power to preach the Gospel. He said he made up his mind that if that were for him he would have it. He said he went home and looked to the Master, and that he never had such a battle with himself in his life. He asked that God would show him the sinfulness of his heart that he knew nothing about, and he just cried mightily to God that he might be emptied of himself and filled with the Spirit, and he said, "God has answered my prayer."

I met him in Edinburgh six months from that date, and he told me he had preached the Gospel every night during that time, that he had not preached one sermon but that some remained for conversation, and that he had engagements four months ahead to preach the Gospel every night in different Churches. I think you could have fired a cannon ball right through his church and not hit anyone before he got this anointing; but it was not thirty days before the building was full and aisles crowded. He had his bucket filled full of fresh water, and the people found it out and came flocking to him from every quarter. I tell you, you can't get the stream higher than the fountain. What we need very specially is power.

There was another man whom I have in my mind, and he said, "I have heart disease, I can't preach more than once a week;" so he had a colleague to preach for him and do the visiting. He was an old minister and couldn't do any visiting. He had heard of this anointing and said, "I would like to be anointed for my burial. I would like before I go hence to have just one more privilege to preach the Gospel with power. He prayed that God would fill him with the Spirit, and I met him not long after that and he said, "I have preached on an average eight times a week, and I have had conversions all along." The Spirit came on him. I don't believe that man broke down at first with hard work, so much as with using the machinery without oil, without lubrication. It is not that the hard word breaks down ministers, but it is the toil of working without power. Oh, that God may anoint His people! Not the ministry only, but every disciple. Do not suppose pastors are the only laborers needing it. There is not a mother but needs it in her house to regulate her family, just as much as the minister needs it in the pulpit or the Sunday-school teacher needs it in his Sunday school. We all need it together and let us not rest day nor night until we possess it. If that is the uppermost thought in our hearts, God will give it to us if we just hunger and thirst for it, and say "God helping me, I will not rest until endued with power from on high."

Master and Servant

There is a very sweet story of Elijah and Elisha in the second chapter of second Kings, and I love to dwell upon it. The time had come for Elijah to be taken up, and he said to Elisha, *"You stay here at Gilgal, and I will go up to Bethel."* There was a theological seminary there, and some young students, and he wanted to see how they were getting along; but Elisha said, *"As the Lord lives, and your soul lives, I will not leave you."* And so Elisha just kept close to Elijah. They came to Bethel, and the sons of the prophets came out and said to Elisha, *"Do you know that your master is to be taken away?"* And Elisha said, *"I know it; but you keep still."* Then Elijah said to Elisha, *"You remain at Bethel until I go to Jericho."* But Elisha said, *"As the Lord lives and my soul lives, I will not leave you."*

"You shall not go without me," says Elisha; and then I can imagine that Elisha just put his arm in that of Elijah, and they walked down together. I can see those two mighty men walking down to Jericho, and when they arrived there, the sons of the prophets came and said to Elisha, *"Do you know that your master is to be taken away?"* *"Hush! keep still,"* says Elisha, *"I know it."* And then Elijah said to Elisha, *"Stay here awhile; for the Lord has sent me to Jordan."* But Elisha said, *"As the Lord lives and my soul lives, I will not leave you."* *"You shall not go without me."* And then Elisha came right close to Elijah, and as they went walking down, I imagine Elisha was after something.

When they came to the Jordan, Elijah took off his mantle and struck the waters, and they separated hither and thither, and the two passed through like giants, dry shod, and fifty sons of the prophets came to look at them and watch them. They didn't know but Elijah would be taken up right in their sight. As they passed over Jordan, Elijah said to Elisha, *"Now, what do you want?"* He knew he was after something. *"What can I do for you? Just make your request known."* And he said, *"I would like a double portion of your Spirit."* I can imagine now that Elijah had given him a chance to ask; he said to himself, *"I will ask for enough."* Elisha had a good deal of the Spirit, but, he says, *"I want a double portion of your Spirit."* *"Well,"* says Elijah, *"if you see me when I am taken up. you shall have it."*

Do you think you could have enticed Elisha from Elijah at that moment? I can almost see the two arm in arm, walking along, and as they walked, there came along the chariot of fire, and before Elisha knew it, Elijah was caught up, and as he went sweeping towards the throne, the servant cried, *"My Father! My Father! The chariot of Israel and the horsemen thereof!"* Elisha saw him no more. He picked up Elijah's fallen mantle, and returning with that old mantle of his master's, he came to the Jordan and cried for Elijah's God, and the waters separated hither and thither, and he passed through dry-shod. Then the watching prophets lifted up their voices and said, *"The Spirit of Elijah is upon Elisha;"* and so it was, a double portion of it.

May the Spirit of Elijah, beloved reader, be upon us. If we seek for it we will have it. Oh, may the God of Elijah answer by fire, and consume the spirit of worldliness in the churches, burn up the dross, and make us whole-hearted Christians. May that Spirit come upon us; let that be our prayer in our family altars and in our closets. Let us cry mightily to God that we may have double portion of the Holy Spirit, and that we may not rest satisfied with this worldly state of living, but let us, like Sampson, shake ourselves and come out from the world, that we may have the POWER OF GOD.

121

CHAPTER 3

Witnessing in Power

The subject of witness-bearing in the power of the Holy Ghost is not sufficiently understood by the Church. Until we have more intelligence on this point we are laboring under great disadvantage. Now, if you will take your Bible and turn to the 15th chapter of John and the 26th verse, you will find these words:

> *"But when the Comforter is come, whom I will send unto you from the Father, even the Spirit of Truth, which proceeds from the Father, He shall testify of me; and you also shall bear witness, because you have been with me from the beginning."*

Here we find what the Spirit is going to do, or what Christ said He would do when He came— namely, that He should testify of Him. And if you will turn over to the second chapter of Acts you will find that when Peter stood up on the day of Pentecost, and testified of what Christ had done, the Holy Spirit came down and bore witness to that fact, and men were convicted by hundreds and by thousands. So then man cannot preach effectively of himself. He must have the Spirit of God to give ability, and study God's Word in order to testify according to the mind of the Spirit.

What is Testimony?

If we keep back the Gospel of Christ and do not bring Christ before the people, then the Spirit has not the opportunity to work. But the moment Peter stood up on the day of Pentecost and bore testimony to this one fact, that Christ died for sin, and that He had been raised again, and ascended into heaven—the Spirit came down to bear witness to the Person and Work of Christ.

He came down to bear witness to the fact that Christ was in heaven, and if it was not for the Holy Ghost bearing witness to the preaching of the facts of the Gospel, do you think that the Church would have lived during these last eighteen centuries? Do you believe that Christ's death, resurrection and ascension would not have been forgotten as soon as His birth, if it had not been for the fact that the Holy Spirit had come? Because it is very clear, that when John made his appearance on the borders of the wilderness, they had forgotten all about the birth of Jesus Christ. Just thirty short years. It was all gone. They had forgotten the story of the Shepherds. They had forgotten the wonderful scene that took place in the temple, when the Son of God was brought into the temple and the older prophets and prophetesses were there. They had forgotten about the wise men coming to Jerusalem to inquire where He was that was born King of the Jews. That story of His birth seemed to have just faded away. They had forgotten all about it, and when John made his appearance on the borders of the wilderness it was brought back to their minds. And if it had not been for the Holy Ghost coming down to bear witness to Christ, to testify of His death and resurrection, these facts would have been forgotten as soon as His birth.

Greater Work

The witness of the Spirit is the witness of power. Jesus said, *"The works that I do you shall do also, and greater works than these you shall do because I go to the Father."* I used to stumble over that. I didn't understand it. I thought, what greater work could any man do than what Christ had done? How could anyone raise a dead man who had been laid away in the sepulcher for days, and who had already begun to turn back to dust. How with a word could he call him forth? But the longer I live the more I am convinced it is a greater thing to influence a man's will; a man whose will is set against God; to have that will broken and brought into subjection to God's will—or, in other words, it is a greater thing to have power over a living, sinning, God hating man, than to quicken the dead. He who could create a world could speak a dead soul into life; but I think the greatest miracle this world has ever seen was the miracle at Pentecost. Here were men who surrounded the Apostles, full of prejudice, full of malice, full of bitterness, their hands, as it were, dripping with the blood of the Son of God, and yet an unlettered man, a man whom they detested, a man whom they hated, stands up there and preaches the Gospel, and three thousand of them are immediately convicted and converted, and become disciples of the Lord Jesus Christ, and are willing to lay down their lives for the Son of God. It may have been on that occasion that Stephen was converted, the first martyr, and some of the men who soon after gave up their lives for Christ.

This seems to me the greatest miracle this world has ever seen. But Peter did not labor alone, the Spirit of God was with him, hence the marvelous results.

The Jewish law required that there should be two witnesses, and so we find that when Peter preached there was a second witness. Peter testified of Christ, and Christ says when the Holy Spirit comes He will testify of Me. And they both bore witness to the verities of our Lord's incarnation, ministry, death, and resurrection, and the result was that a multitude turned as with one heart unto the Lord. Our failure now is, that preachers ignore the Cross, and veil Christ with samples sermons and superfine language. They don't just present Him to the people plainly, and that is why, I believe, that the Spirit of God doesn't work with power in our churches. What we need is to preach Christ and present Him to a perishing world. The world can get on very well without you and me, but the world cannot get on without Christ, and therefore we must testify of Him, and the world, I believe, today is just hungering and thirsting for this divine, satisfying portion. Thousands and thousands are sitting in darkness, knowing not of this great Light, but when we begin to preach Christ honestly, faithfully, sincerely and truthfully; holding Him up, not ourselves; exalting Christ and not our theories; presenting Christ and not our opinions; advocating Christ and not some false doctrine; then the Holy Ghost will come and bear witness. He will testify that what we say is true. When He comes He will confirm the Word with signs following.

This is one of the strongest proofs that our Gospel is Divine; that it is of Divine origin; that not only did Christ teach these things, but when leaving the World He said, "He shall glorify Me," and "He will testify of Me." If you will just look at the second chapter of Acts—to that wonderful sermon that Peter preached—the thirty-sixth verse, you read these words: "Therefore let all the house of Israel know assuredly that God has made that same

Jesus whom you crucified, both Lord and Christ." And when Peter said this the Holy Ghost descended upon the people and testified of Christ—bore witness in signal demonstration that all this was true. And again, in the fortieth verse, *"And with many other words did He testify and exhort, saying, Save yourselves from this perverse generation."* With many other words did He testify, not only these words that have been recorded, but many other words.

The Sure Guide

Turn to the sixteenth chapter of John, in the thirteenth verse, and read:

> *"Howbeit, when He, the Spirit of Truth is come, He will guide you into all truth; for He shall not speak of Himself; but whatsoever He shall hear that shall He speak; and He will show you things to come. He will guide you into all truth."*

Now there is not a truth that we ought to know but the Spirit of God will guide us into it if we will let Him; if we will yield ourselves up to be directed by the Spirit, and let Him lead us, He will guide us into all truth.

It would have saved us from a great many dark hours if we had only been willing to let the Spirit of God be our counselor and guide. Lot never would have gone to Sodom if he had been guided by the Spirit of God. David never would have fallen into sin and had all that trouble with his family if he had been guided by the Spirit of God.

There are many Lots and Davids now-a-days. The churches are full of them. Men and women are in total darkness, because they have not been willing to be guided by the Spirit of God. *"He shall guide you into all truth. He shall not speak of Himself."* He shall speak of the ascended glorified Christ.

What would be thought of a messenger, entrusted by an absent husband with a message for his wife or mother who, on arrival, only talked of himself, and his conceits, and ignored both the husband and the message? You would simply call it outrageous. What then must be the crime of the professed teacher who speaks of himself, or some insipid theory, leaving out Christ and His Gospel? If we witness according to the Spirit, we must witness of Jesus.

The Holy Spirit is down here in this dark world to just speak of the Absent One, and He takes the things of Christ and brings them to our mind. He testifies of Christ. He guides us into the truth about Him.

Rappings in the Dark

I want to say right here, that I think in this day a great many children of God are turning aside and committing a grievous sin. I don't know as they think it is a sin, but if we examine the Scriptures, I am sure we will find that it is a great sin. We are told that the Comforter is sent into the world to *"guide us into all truth,"* and if He is sent for that purpose, do we need any other guide? Need we hide in the darkness, consulting with mediums, which profess to call up the spirits of the dead Do you know what the Word of God pronounces against that fearful sin? I believe it is one of the greatest sins we have to contend with at the present day. It is dishonoring to the Holy Spirit for me to go and summon up the dead and confer with them, even if it were possible.

I would like you to notice the 10th chapter of 1st Chronicles, and 13th verse:

"So Saul died for his transgression which he had committed against the Lord, even against the Word of the Lord, which he kept not, and also for asking counsel of one that had a familiar spirit, to inquire of it; and inquired not of the Lord: therefore He slew him, and turned the kingdom unto David the son of Jesse."

God slew him for this very sin. Of the two sins that are brought against Saul here, one is that he would not listen to the Word of God, and the second is that he consulted a familiar spirit. He was snared by this great evil, and sinned against God.

Saul fell right here, and there are a great many of God's professed children today who think there is no harm in consulting a medium that pretends to call up some of the departed to inquire of them. But how dishonoring it is to God who has sent the Holy Spirit into this world to guide us "into all truth." There is not a thing that I need to know, there is not a thing that is important for me to know. There is not a thing that I ought to know but the Spirit of God will reveal it to me through the Word of God, and if I turn my back upon the Holy Spirit, I am dishonoring the Spirit of God, and I am committing a grievous sin. You know we read in Luke, where that rich man in the other world wanted to have someone sent to his father's house to warn his five brothers, Christ said *"They have Moses and the prophets, and if they will not hear them, they will not hear one though he rose from the dead."* Moses and the prophets, the part of the Bible then completed, that is enough. But a great many people now want something besides the Word of God, and are turning aside to these false lights.

Spirits That Peep and Mutter

There is another passage which reads:

"And when they shall say unto you, seek unto them that have familiar spirits, and unto wizards that peep and mutter: Should not a people seek unto their God? For the living to the dead?" (Isa. 8:19).

What is but table-rapping, and cabinet-hiding? If it was a message from God, do you think you would have to go into a dark room and put out all the lights? In secret my Master taught nothing. God is not in that movement, and what we want, as children of God, is to keep ourselves from this evil. And then notice the verse following, quoted so often out of its connection: *"... to the law and to the testimony; if they speak not according to this word, it is because there is no light in them."* Any man, any woman, who comes to us with any doctrine that is not according to the law and the testimony, let us understand that they are from the evil one, and that they are enemies of righteousness. They have no light in them. Now you will find these people who are consulting familiar spirits, first and last, attack the Word of God. They don't believe it. Still a great many people say, you must hear both sides. But if a man should write me a most slanderous letter about my wife, I don't think I would have to read it. I would tear it up and throw it to the winds. Do I have to read all the infidel books that are written, to hear both sides? Do I have to take up a book that is a slander on my Lord and Master, who has redeemed me with His blood? Ten thousand times, No. I will not touch it.

"Now the Spirit speaks expressly, that in the latter times some shall depart from the faith, giving heed to seducing spirits, and doctrines of devils" (1 Timothy 4:1).

That is pretty plain language, isn't it? *"Doctrines of devils."* Again, *"speaking lies in hypocrisy; having their consciences seared with a hot iron."* There are other passages of Scripture warning against every delusion of Satan. Let us ever remember the Spirit has been sent into the world to guide us into all truth. We don't want any other guide; He is enough. Some people say, "Is not conscience a safer guide than the Word and the Spirit?" No, it is not. Some people don't seem to have any conscience, and don't know what it means. Their education has a good deal to do with conscience. There are persons who will say that their conscience did not tell them that they had done wrong until after the wrong was done; but what we want, is something to tell us a thing is wrong before we do it.

Very often a man will go and commit some awful crime, and after it is done his conscience will wake up and lash and scourge him, and then it is too late, the act is done.

The Unerring Guide

I am told by people who have been over the Alps, that the guide fastens them, if they are going in a dangerous place, right to himself, and he just goes on before: they

131

are fastened to the guide. And so should the Christian be linked to His unerring Guide, and be safely upheld. Why if a man is going through the Mammoth Cave, it would be death to him if he strayed away from his guide—if he separated from him, he would certainly perish. There are pitfalls in that cave and a bottomless river, and there would be no chance for a man to find his way through that cave without a guide or light.

So there is no chance for us to get through the dark wilderness of this world alone. It is folly for a man or woman to think that they can get through this evil world without the light of God's Word and the guidance of the Divine Spirit. God sent Him to guide us through this great journey, and if we seek to work independent of Him, we shall stumble into the deep darkness of eternity's night. But bear in mind the Words of the Spirit of God; if you want to be guided, you must study the Word; because the Word is the light of the Spirit. In the 14th chapter of John and 26th verse, we read:

"But the Comforter, which is the Holy Ghost, whom the Father will send in my name, He shall teach you all things, and bring all things to your remembrance, whatsoever I have said unto you."

Again in John 16:13:

"Howbeit when he, the Spirit of truth, is come, he will guide you into all truth: for he shall not speak of himself; but whatsoever he shall hear, that shall he speak: and he will show you things to come."

A great many people seem to think that the Bible is out of date, that it is an old book, and they think it has passed its day. They say it was very good for the dark ages, and that there is some very good history in it; but then it was not intended for the present time. They say we are living in a very enlightened age, and that men can get on very well without the old book; that we have outgrown it. They think we have no use for it, because is an old book. Now you might just as well say that the sun, which has shone so long, is now so old that it is out of date, and that whenever a man builds a house he need not put any windows in it, because we now have a newer light and a better light. We have gaslight and this new electric light. These are new things; and I would advise people, if they think the Bible is too old and worn out, when they build houses, not to put any windows in them, but just to light them with this new electric light; that is something new, and this is what they are anxious for.

People talk about this Book as if they understood it, but we don't know much about it yet. The press gives us the daily news of what has taken place. This Bible, however, tells us what is about to take place. This is new; we have the news here in this Book. It tells us of the things that will surely come to pass, and that is a great deal newer than anything in the newspapers. It tells us that the Spirit shall teach us all things; not only guide us into all truth, but teach us all things. He teaches us how to pray, and I don't think there has ever been a prayer upon this sin-cursed earth that has been indicted by the Holy Spirit but was answered. There is much praying that is not indicted by the Holy Spirit. In former years I was very ambitious to get rich. I used to pray for one hundred thousand dollars; that was my aim, and I used to say, "God does not answer my prayer; He does not make me rich." But I had no warrant for such a prayer. Yet a good many people pray in that way. They think that they pray, but they do not pray according to the Scriptures. The Spirit of God has nothing to do with their prayers, and such prayers are not the product of His teaching.

It is the Spirit who teaches us how to answer our enemies. If a man strikes me, I should not pull out a revolver and shoot him. The Spirit of the Lord doesn't teach me revenge. He doesn't teach me that it is necessary to draw the sword and cut a man down in order to defend my rights. Some people say, "You are a coward if you don't strike back." Christ says, *"turn the other cheek to him who smites."* I would rather take Christ's teaching than any other. I don't think a man gains much by loading himself down with weapons to defend himself. There has been life enough sacrificed in this country to teach men a lesson in this regard. The Word of God is a much better protection than the revolver. We better take the Word of God to protect us, by accepting it's teaching, and living out its precepts.

An Aid to Memory

It is a great comfort to us to remember that another office of the Spirit is to bring the teaching of Jesus to our remembrance. This was our Lord's promise, *"He shall teach you all things, and bring all things to your remembrance."* John 16:26 How striking that is. I think there are many Christians who have had that experience. They have been testifying, and found that while talking for Christ the Spirit has just brought into mind some of the sayings of the Lord Jesus Christ, and their mind was soon filled with the Word of God.

When we have the Spirit resting upon us, we can speak with authority and power, and the Lord will bless our testimony and bless our work. I believe the reason why God makes use of so few in the Church, is because there is not in them the power that God can use. He is not going to use our ideas, but we must have the Word of God hid in our hearts, and then, the Holy Spirit inflaming us, we will have the testimony that will be rich, and sweet, and fresh, and the Lord's Word will vindicate itself in blessed results. God wants to use us! God wants to make us channels of blessing, but we are in such a condition He does not use us. That is the trouble. There are so many men who have no testimony for the Lord. If they speak, they speak without saying anything, and if they pray, their prayer is powerless. They do not plead in prayer; their prayer is just a few set phrases that you have heard too often. Now what we want is to be so full of the Word, that the Spirit coming upon us shall bring to mind—bring to our remembrance—the words of the Lord Jesus.

In 1 Corinthians 2:9 it is written:

"Eye has not seen, nor ear heard, neither have entered into the heart of man, the things which God has prepared for them that love him."

We hear that quoted so often in prayer. Many a man weaves it into his prayer and stops right there. And the moment you talk about Heaven, they say, "Oh, we don't know anything about Heaven; it has not entered into the heart of man; eye has not seen; it is all speculation; we have nothing to do with it; and they say they quote it as it is written. *"Eye has not seen, nor ear heard, neither have entered into the heart of man, the things which God has prepared for them that love him."* What next? ***"But God*** *has revealed them unto us by His Spirit."* You see the Lord has revealed them unto us: *"For the Spirit searches all things—yea, the deep things of God."* That is just what the Spirit does.

Long and Short Sight

He brings to our mind what God has in store for us. I heard a man, some time ago, speaking about Abraham. He said "Abraham was not tempted by the well-watered plains of Sodom, for Abraham was what you might call a long-sighted man. He had his eyes set on the city which had foundation—'whose Builder and Maker is God.'" But Lot was a short-sighted man, and there are many people in the Church who are very short sighted. They only see things right around them they think are good. Abraham was long-sighted, and he had glimpses of the celestial city. Moses was long-sighted, and he left the palaces of Egypt and identified himself with God's people—poor people, who were slaves. But he had something in view yonder; he could see something God had in store. Again there are some people who are sort of long-sighted and short-sighted, too. I have a friend who has one eye that is long-sighted and the other is short-sighted, and I think the Church is full of this kind of people. They want one eye for the world and the other for the Kingdom of God. Therefore, everything is blurred, one eye is long and the other is short, all is confusion, and they "see men as trees walking." The Church is filled with that sort of people.

But Stephen was long-sighted. He looked clear into heaven. They couldn't convince him even when he was dying, that Christ had not ascended to heaven. *"Look, look yonder,"* he says, *"I see Him over there; He is on the throne, standing at the right hand of God;"* and he looked clear into heaven; the world had no temptation for him; he had put the world under his feet.

Paul was another of those long-sighted men. He had been caught up and seen things unlawful for him to utter—things grand and glorious. I tell you when the Spirit of God is on us the world looks very empty. The world has a very small hold upon us, and we begin to let go our hold of it. When the Spirit of God is on us we will just let go the things of time and lay hold of things eternal. This is the Church's need today. We want the Spirit to come in mighty power, and consume all the vile dross there is in us. Oh, that the Spirit of fire may come down and burn everything in us that is contrary to God's blessed Word and Will.

In John 14:16, we read of the Comforter. This is the first time He is spoken of as the Comforter. Christ had been their Comforter. God had sent Him to comfort the sorrowing. It was prophesied of Him, *"The Spirit of the Lord is upon me, because He has anointed me to preach the Gospel to the poor; He has sent me to heal the broken hearted."* You can't heal the broken-hearted without the Comforter. But the world would not have the first Comforter, and so they rose up and took Him to Calvary and put Him to death; but on going away He said:

> *"I will send you another Comforter; you shall not be comfortless; be of good cheer, little flock; it is the Father's good pleasure to give you the kingdom."*

All these sweet passages are brought to the remembrance of God's people, and they help us to rise out of the fog and mist of this world. O, what a comforter is the Holy Spirit of God!

The Faithful Friend

The Holy Spirit tells a man of his faults in order to lead him to a better life. In John 16:8 we read:

"He is to reprove the world of sin."

Now, there are a class of people who don't like this part of the Spirit's work. Do you know why? Because He convicts them of sin, and they don't like that. What they want is someone to speak comforting words and make everything pleasant; keep everything all quiet; tell them there is peace when there is war; tell them it is light when it is dark, and tell them everything is growing better. They want someone to tell them that the world is getting on amazingly in goodness; that it is growing better all the time; that is the kind of preaching they seek for.

Men think they are a great deal better than their fathers were. That suits human nature, for it is full of pride. Men will strut around and say, "Yes, I believe that; the world is improving; I am a good deal better man than father was; my father was too strict; he was one of those old Puritanical men who was so rigid. O, we are getting on; we are more liberal; my father wouldn't think of going out riding on Sunday, but we will. We will trample the laws of God under our feet; we are better than our fathers." This is the kind of preaching that some dearly love, and there are preachers who tickle such itching ears. When you bring the Word of God to bear upon them, and when the Spirit drives it home, then men will say: "I don't like that kind of preaching; I will never go to hear that man again;" and sometimes they will get up and stamp their way out of church before the speaker gets through, because they don't like it. But when the Spirit of God is at work he convicts men of sin. *"When He comes He will reprove the world of sin, of righteousness and of judgment; of sin"*—not because men swear and lie and steal and get drunk and murder—*"of sin because they believe not on Me."*

The Climax Sin

That is the sin of the world. Why, a great many people think that unbelief is a sort of misfortune, but do not know, if you will allow me the expression, it is the damning sin of the world today; that is what unbelief is, the mother of all sin. There would not be a drunkard walking the streets, if it were not for unbelief. There would not be a harlot walking the streets, if it were not for unbelief. There would not be a murderer, if it were not for unbelief; it is the germ of all sin. Don't think for a moment that it is a misfortune, but just bear in mind it is an awful sin, and may the Holy Spirit convict every reader that unbelief is making God a liar. Many a man has been knocked down on the streets because some one has told him he was a liar. Unbelief is giving God the lie; that is the plain English of it.

Some people seem to boast of their unbelief. They seem to think it is quite respectable to be an infidel and doubt God's Word, and they will vainly boast and say, "I have intellectual difficulties; I can't believe." Oh that the Spirit of God may come and convict men of sin! That is what we need—His convicting power, and I am so thankful that God has not put that into our hands. We have not to convict men; if we had I would get discouraged, and give up preaching, and go back to business within the next forty-eight hours. It is my work to preach and hold up the Cross and testify of Christ; but it is His work to convict men of sin and lead them to Christ.

One thing I have noticed is that some conversions don't amount to anything. If a man professes to be converted without conviction of sin, he is one of those stony-ground hearers who don't bring forth much fruit. The first little wave of persecution, the first breath of opposition, and the man is back in the world again. Let us pray, dear Christian reader, that God may carry on a deep and thorough work, that men may be convicted of sin so that they cannot rest in unbelief. Let us pray God it may be a thorough work in the land. I would a great deal rather see a hundred men thoroughly converted, truly born of God, than to see a thousand professed conversions where the Spirit of God has not convicted of sin. Don't let us cry, "Peace, peace, when there is no peace." Don't go to the man who is living in sin, and tell him all he has to do is to stand right up and profess, without any hatred for sin. Let us ask God first to show every man the plague of his own heart, that the Spirit, may convict them of sin. Then will the work in our hands be real, and deep, and abide the fiery trial which will try every man's labor.

Thus far, we have found the work of the Spirit is to impart life, to implant hope, to give liberty, to testify of Christ, to guide us into all truth, to teach us all things, to comfort the believers, and to convict the world of sin.

CHAPTER 4

Power in Operation

The power we have been considering is the Presence of The Holy Spirit. He is omnipotent. Power in operation is the actions of the Spirit or the fruit of the Spirit. This we shall now consider.

Paul writes in Galatians 5:16:

"This I say then, walk in the Spirit, and you shall not fulfill the lust of the flesh. For the flesh lusts against the Spirit, and the Spirit against the flesh; and these are contrary, the one to the other; so that you cannot do the things that you would. But if you are led of the Spirit, you are not under the law. But the fruit of the Spirit is love, joy, peace, longsuffering, gentleness, goodness, faith, meekness, temperance; against such there is not law. And they that are Christ's have crucified the flesh with the affections and lusts. If we live in the Spirit, let us also walk in the Spirit. Let us not be desirous of vain glory, provoking one another, envying one another."

Now there is a life of perfect peace, perfect joy, and perfect love, and that ought to be the aim of every child of God; that ought to be their standard; and they should not rest until having attained to that position. That is God's standard, where He wants all His children. These nine graces mentioned in this chapter in Galatians can be divided in this way: Love and peace and joy are all to God. God looks for that fruit from each one of His children, and that is the kind of fruit that is acceptable with Him. Without that we cannot please God. He wants, above everything else that we possess, love, peace and joy. And then the next three; goodness, longsuffering and gentleness; are towards man. That is our outward life to those that we are coming in contact with continually—daily, hourly. The next three; faith, temperance, meekness; are in relation to ourselves; and in that way we can just take the three divisions, and it will be of some help to us. The first thing that meets us as we enter the kingdom of God, you might say, is these first three graces: Love, Peace, and Joy.

When a man who has been living in sin turns from his sins, and turns to God with all his heart, he is met on the threshold of the divine life by these sister graces. The love of God is shed abroad in his heart by the Holy Ghost. The peace of God comes at the same time, and also the joy of the Lord. We can put the test to ourselves, if we have them. It is not anything that we can make. The great trouble with many is that they are trying to make these graces. They are trying to make love; they are trying to make peace; they are trying to make joy. But they are not creatures of human planting. To produce them of ourselves is impossible. That is an act of God. They come from above. It is God who speaks the word and gives the love; it is God who gives the peace; and we possess all by receiving Jesus Christ by faith into the heart. When Christ comes by faith into the heart then the Spirit is there, and if we have the Spirit we will have the fruit.

If the whole Church of God could live as the Lord would have them live, why Christianity would be the mightiest power this world has ever seen. It is the low standard of Christian life that is causing so much trouble.

There are a great many stunted Christians in the Church; their lives are stunted; they are like a tree planted in poor soil—the soil is hard and stony, and the roots cannot find the rich loamy soil needed. Such believers have not grown in these sweet graces. Peter, in his second epistle, 1st chapter and 5th verse, writes:

"And beside this, giving all diligence, add to your faith virtue; and to virtue knowledge; and to knowledge temperance; and to temperance patience; and to patience godliness; and to godliness brotherly kindness; and to brotherly kindness charity. For if these things be in you, and abound, they make you that you shall neither be barren nor unfruitful in the knowledge of our Lord Jesus Christ."

Now, if we have these things in us, I believe that we will be constantly bringing forth fruit that will be acceptable with God. It won't be just a little every now and then, when we spur ourselves up and work ourselves up into a certain state of mind or into an excited condition, and work a little while and then become cold, and discouraged, and disheartened. We shall be neither unfruitful nor barren, bringing forth fruit constantly, we will grow in grace and be filled with the Spirit of God.

What Wins

A great many parents have inquired of me how to win their children. They say they have talked with them, and sometimes they have scolded them and have lectured them, and thoroughly failed. I think there is no way so sure to win our families and our neighbors, and those about whom we are anxious, to Christ, than just to adorn the doctrine of Jesus Christ in our lives, and grow in all these graces. If we have peace and joy and love and gentleness and goodness and temperance; not only being temperate in what we drink, but in what we eat, and temperate in our language, guarded in our expressions; if we just live in our homes as the Lord would have us, an even Christian life day by day, we shall have a quiet and silent power proceeding from us, that will constrain them to believe on the Lord Jesus Christ. But an uneven life, hot today and cold tomorrow, will only repel.

Many are watching God's people. It is just the very worst thing that can happen to those whom we want to win to Christ, to see us, at any time, in a cold, backslidden state. This is not the normal condition of the Church; it is not God's intention. He would have us growing in all these graces, and the only true, happy, Christian life is to be growing, constantly growing in the love and favor of God, growing in all those delightful graces of the Spirit.

Even the vilest, the most impure, acknowledge the power of goodness; they recognize the fruit of the Spirit. It may condemn their lives and cause them to say bitter things at times, but down deep in their hearts they know that the man or woman who is living that kind of life, is superior to them. The world doesn't satisfy them, and if we can show the world that Jesus Christ does satisfy us in our present life, it will be more powerful than the eloquent words of professional reformers. A man may preach with the eloquence of an angel, but if he doesn't live what he preaches, and act out in his home and his business what he professes, his testimony goes for naught, and the people say it is all hypocrisy after all; it is all a sham.

Words are very empty, if there is nothing to back them. Your testimony is poor and worthless, if there is not a record behind that testimony consistent with what you profess. What we need is to pray to God to lift us up out of this low, cold, formal state that we have been living in, that we may live in the atmosphere of God continually, and that the Lord may lift upon us the light of his countenance, and that we may shine in this world, reflecting His grace and glory.

The first of the graces spoken of in Galatians, and the last mentioned in Peter, is charity or love. We cannot serve God, we cannot work for God unless we have love. That is the key that unlocks the human heart. If I can prove to a man that I come to him out of pure love; if a mother shows by her actions that it is pure love that prompts her advising her boy to lead a different life, not a selfish love, but that it is for the glory of God, it won't be long before that mother's influence will be felt by that boy, and he will begin to think about this matter, because true love touches the heart quicker than anything else.

Power of Love

Love is the badge that Christ gave His disciples. Some put on one sort of badge and some another. Some put on a strange kind of dress, that they might be known as Christians, and some put on a crucifix, or something else, that they might be known as Christians. But love is the only badge by which the disciples of our Lord Jesus Christ are known. *"By this shall all men know that you are My disciples, if you have love one toward another."* Therefore, though a man stand before an audience and speak with the eloquence of a Demosthenes, or of the greatest living orator, if there is no love back of his words, it is like sounding brass and a tinkling cymbal. I would recommend all Christians to read the thirteenth chapter of First Corinthians constantly, abiding in it day and night, not spending a night or a day there, but just go in there and spend all our time—summer and winter, twelve months in the year, then the power of Christ and Christianity would be felt as it never has been in the history of the world.

See what this chapter says:

"Though I speak with the tongues of men and of angels, and have not love, I have become as sounding brass, or a tinkling cymbal. And though I have the gift of prophecy, and understand all mysteries, and all knowledge; and though I have all faith, so that I could remove mountains, and have not love, I am nothing." A great many are praying for faith; they want extra ordinary faith; they want remarkable faith. They forget that love exceeds faith. The Charity spoken of in the above verses, is LOVE, The fruit of the Spirit, the great motive-power of life. What the Church of God needs today is love—more love to God and more love to our fellow-men. If we love God more, we will love our fellow-men more. There is no doubt about that. I used to think that I would like to have lived in the days of the prophets; that I should like

to have been one of the prophets, to prophesy, and to see the beauties of heaven and describe them to men; but as I understand the Scriptures now, I would a good deal rather live in the thirteenth chapter of 1st Corinthians and have this love that Paul is speaking of, the love of God burning in my soul like an unquenchable flame, so that I may reach men and win them for heaven.

A man may have wonderful knowledge, that may unravel the mysteries of the Bible, and yet be as cold as an icicle. He may glisten like the snow in the sun. Sometimes you have wondered why it was that certain ministers who have had such wonderful magnetism, who have such a marvelous command of language, and who preach with such mental strength, haven't had more conversions. I believe, if the truth be known, you would find no divine love behind their words, no pure love in their sermons. You may preach like an angel, Paul says, *"with the tongues of men and of angels,"* but if you have not love, it amounts to nothing. *"And though I bestow all my goods to feed the poor"*—a man may be very charitable and give away all his goods, a man may give all he has—but if it is not the love of God which prompts the gift, it will not be acceptable to God. *"And though I give my body to be burned, and have not love it profits me nothing."* A man may go to the stake for his principles; he may go to the stake for what he believes, but if it is not love to God that actuates him, it will not be acceptable to God.

Love's Wonderful Effects

In Paul's first epistle to the Corinthians, in the thirteenth chapter we read:

"Love suffers long, and is kind; love envies not; love exalts not itself, is not puffed up; does not behave itself unseemly, seeks not her own, is not easily provoked, thinks no evil."

That's the work of love. It is not easily provoked. Now if a man has no love of God in his heart, how easy it is to become offended. Perhaps with the church because some members of the church don't treat him just right, or some men of the church don't bow to him on the street, he takes offense, and that is the last you see of him. Love is long-suffering. If I love the Lord Jesus Christ, these little things are not going to separate me from His people. They are like the dust in the balance. Nor will the cold, formal treatment of hypocrites in the church quench that love I have in my heart for Him. If this love is in the heart, and the fire is burning on the altar, we will not be all the time finding fault with other people and criticizing what they have done.

Critics Beware!

Love will rebuke evil, but will not rejoice in it. Love will be impatient of sin, but patient with the sinner. To form the habit of finding fault constantly, is very damaging to spiritual life. It is about the lowest and meanest position that a man can take. I never saw a man who was aiming to do the best work, but there could have been some improvement; I never did anything in my life, I never addressed an audience, that I didn't think I could have done better. And I have often upbraided myself that I had not done better. But to sit down and find fault with other people when we are doing nothing ourselves, not lifting our hands to save someone, is all wrong, and is the opposite of holy, patient, divine love.

Love is forbearance, and what we want is to get this spirit of criticism and fault finding out of the Church and out of our hearts. Let each one of us live as if we had to answer for ourselves, and not for the community, at the last day. If we are living according to the 13th chapter of Corinthians, we will not be all the time finding fault with other people. *"Love suffers long, and is kind."*

Love forgets itself, and doesn't dwell upon itself. The woman who came to Christ with that alabaster box, I venture to say, never thought of herself. Little did she know what an act she was performing. It was just her love for the Master. She forgot the surroundings, she forgot everything else that was there; she broke that box and poured the ointment upon Him, and filled the house with its odor. The act, as a memorial, has come down these 1800 years. It is right here—the perfume of that box is in the world today. The ointment was worth $40 or $50; no small sum of those days for a poor woman. Judas sold the Son of God for about $15 or $20. But what this woman gave to Christ was everything that she had, and she became so occupied with Jesus Christ that she didn't think what people were going to say. So when we act with a single eye for the glory of our Lord, not finding fault with everything about us, but doing what we can in the power of this love, then will our deeds for God speak, and the world will acknowledge that we have been with Jesus, and that this glorious love has been shed abroad in our hearts.

If we don't love the Church of God, I am afraid it won't do us much good. If we don't love the blessed Bible, it will not do us much good. What we want, then, is to have love for Christ, to have love for His Word, and to have love for the Church of God, and when we have love, and are living in that spirit, we will not be in the spirit of finding fault and working mischief.

After Love, What?

After love comes peace. I have before remarked, a great many people are trying to make peace. But that has already been done. God has not left it for us to do; all that we have to do is to enter into it. It is a condition, and instead of our trying to make peace and to work for peace, we want to cease all that, and sweetly enter into peace.

If I discover a man in the cellar complaining because there is no light there, and because it is cold and damp, I say: "My friend, come up out of the cellar. There is a good warm sun up here, a beautiful spring day, and it is warm, it is cheerful and light. Come up, and enjoy it." Would he reply, "O, no, sir; I am trying to see if I can make light down here. I am trying to work myself into a warm feeling." And there he is working away, and he has been at it for a whole week. I can imagine my reader's smile; but you may be smiling at your own picture; for this is the condition of many whom I daily meet who are trying to do this very thing—they are trying to work themselves into peace and joyful feelings. Peace is a condition into which we enter. It is a state. And instead of our trying to make peace, let us believe what God's Word declares, that peace has already been made by the blood of the Cross. Christ has made peace for us, and now what He desires is that we believe it and enter into it. Now, the only thing that can keep us from peace is sin. God turns the way of the wicked upside down.

There is no peace for the wicked, says my God. They are like the troubled sea that cannot rest, casting up filth and mire all the while; but peace with God by faith in Jesus Christ—peace through knowledge of forgiven sin is like a rock; the waters go dashing and surging past it, but it abides. When we find peace, we shall not find it on the ground of innate goodness; it comes from without ourselves, but into us. In the 16th chapter of John and the 33d verse we read: *"These things have I spoken unto you, that in me you might have peace."* In me you might have peace. Jesus Christ is the author of peace. He procured peace. His gospel is the gospel of peace.

"Behold I bring you good tidings of great joy which shall be unto all people; for unto you is born this day in the city of David a Savior," and then came that chorus from heaven, *"Glory to God in the highest; peace on earth."* He brought peace.

"In the world you shall have tribulation, but be of good cheer, I have overcome the world" (John 16:33). How true that in the world we have tribulation. Are you in tribulation? Are you in trouble? Are you in sorrow? Remember this is our lot. Paul had tribulation, and others shared in grief. Nor shall we be exempt from trial.

But within, peace may reign undisturbed. If sorrow is our lot, peace is our legacy. Jesus gives peace, and do you know there is a good deal of difference between His peace and our peace? Any one can disturb our peace, but they can't disturb His peace. That is the kind of peace He has left us. Nothing can offend those who trust in Christ.

Easily Offended

In the 119th Psalm and the 165th verse, we find:

"Great peace have they who love thy law: and nothing shall offend them."

The study of God's Word will secure peace. You take Christians who are rooted and grounded in the Word of God, and you find they have great peace; but it is these who don't study their Bible, and don't know their Bible, who are easily offended when some little trouble comes, or some little persecution, and their peace is all disturbed; just a little breath of opposition, and their peace is all gone.

Sometimes I am amazed to see how little it takes to drive all peace and comfort from some people, some slandering tongue will readily blast it.

But if we have the peace of God, the world cannot take that from us. It cannot give it. It cannot destroy it. We have to get it from above the world. It is peace that Christ gives. *"Great peace have they which love Your law, and nothing shall offend them."* Christ says, *"Blessed is he, whosoever shall not be offended in Me."* Now, if you will notice, wherever there is a Bible-taught Christian, one who has the Bible well marked, and daily feeds upon the Word by prayerful meditation, he will not be easily offended.

Such are the people who are growing and working all the while. But it is these people who never open their Bibles, these people who never study the Scriptures, who become offended, and are wondering why they are having such a hard time. They are the people who tell you that Christianity is not what it has been recommended to them;

that they have found it was not all that we claim it to be. The real trouble is, they have not done as the Lord has told them to do. They have neglected the Word of God. If they had been studying the Word of God, they would not be in that condition. If they had been studying the Word of God, they would not have wandered these years away from God, living on the husks of the world. But the trouble is, they have neglected to care for the new life; they haven't fed it, and the poor soul, being starved, sinks into weakness and decay, and is easily stumbled or offended.

I met a man who confessed his soul had fed on nothing for forty years. "Well," I said, "that is pretty hard for the soul—giving it nothing to feed on!" And that man is but a type of thousands and tens of thousands today; their poor souls are starving. This body that we inhabit for a day, and then leave, we take good care of; we feed it three times a day, and we clothe it, and take care of it, and deck it, and by and by it is going into the grave to be eaten up by worms. But the inner man, that is live on and on, forever, is lean and starved.

Sweet Words

In the 6th chapter of Numbers and 22d verse we read:

> "And the Lord spoke unto Moses, saying, Speak unto Aaron and unto his sons, saying, On this wise you shall bless the children of Israel, saying unto them, The Lord bless you, and keep you: The Lord make his face shine upon you, and be gracious unto you: The Lord lift up his countenance upon you, and give you peace."

I think these are about as sweet verses as we find in the Old Testament. I marked them years ago in my Bible, and many times I have turned over and read them. *"The Lord life up His countenance upon you, and give you peace."* They remind us of the loving words of Jesus to his troubled disciples. *"Peace, be still."* The Jewish salutation used to be, as a man went into a house, "Peace be upon this house," and as he left the house the host would say, "Go in Peace." Then again, in the 14th chapter of John and the 27th verse, Jesus said:

"Peace I leave with you, my peace I give unto you: not as the world gives, give I unto you. Let not your heart be troubled, neither let it be afraid."

This is the precious legacy of Jesus to all His followers. Every man, every woman, every child, who believes in Him, may share in this portion. Christ has willed it to them and His peace is theirs.

This then is our Lord's purpose and promise. My peace I give unto you. I give it, and I am not going to take it away again; I am going to leave it to you. *"Not as the world gives, give I unto you. Let not your heart be troubled, neither let it be afraid."*

But you know, when some men make their wills and deed away their property, there are some sharp, shrewd lawyers who will get hold of that will and break it all to pieces. They will go into court and break the will, and the jury will set the will aside, and the money goes into another channel. Now this will that Christ has made, neither the devil nor man can break it. He has promised to give us peace, and there are thousands of witnesses who can say: "I have my part of that legacy. I have peace; I came to

Him for peace, and I got it. I came to Him in darkness; I came to Him in trouble and sorrow; I was passing under a deep cloud of affliction, and I came to Him and He said, *'Peace, be still.'* And from that hour peace reigned in my soul." Yes, many have proved the invitation true, *"Come unto Me all you that labor and are heavy laden, and I will give you rest."* They found rest when they came. He is the author of rest, He is the author of peace, and no power can break that will; yea, unbelief may question it, but Jesus Christ rose to execute His own will, and it is in vain for man to contest it.

Infidels and skeptics may tell us that it is all a myth, and that there isn't anything in it, and yet the glorious tidings are ever repeated. *"Peace on earth, good will to man,"* and the poor and needy, the sad and sorrowful, are made partakers of it.

So, my reader, you need not wait for peace any longer. All you have to do is to enter into it today. You need not try to make peace. It is a false idea; you cannot make it. Peace is already made by Jesus Christ, and is now declared unto you.

Peace Declared

When France and England were at war, a French vessel had gone off on a long voyage, a whaling voyage; and when they came back, the crew was short of water. Being now near and English port they wanted to get water, but they were afraid that they would be taken if they went into that port. Some people in the port saw them, saw their signal of distress, and sent word to them that they need not be afraid, that the war was over, and peace had been declared. But they couldn't make those sailors believe it, and they didn't dare to go into port, although they were out of water. At last they made up their minds that they had better go in and surrender up their cargo and surrender up their lives to their enemies than to perish at sea without water.

When they got in, they found out that peace had been declared, and that what had been told them was true. So there are a great many people who don't believe the glad tiding that peace has been made. Jesus Christ made peace on the Cross. He satisfied the claims of the law; and this law that condemns you and me has been fulfilled by Jesus Christ. He has made peace, and now He wants us just to enjoy it, just to believe it. Nor is there a thing to hinder us from doing it, if we will. We can enter into that blessing now, and have perfect peace. The promise is:

"You will keep him in perfect peace whose mind is stayed on you. Trust in the Lord forever, for in the Lord Jehovah is everlasting strength."

Now, as long as our mind is stayed on our dear selves, we will never have peace. Some people think more of themselves than of all the rest of the world. It is self in the morning, self at noon, and self at night. It is self when they wake up, and self when they go to bed; and they are all the time looking at themselves and thinking about themselves, instead of "looking unto Jesus" Faith is an outward look. Faith does not look within; it looks without. It is not what I think, nor what I feel, nor what I have done, but it is what Jesus Christ is and has done, and so we should trust in Him who is our strength, and whose strength will never fail. After Christ rose from the grave, three times, John tells us, He met His disciples and said unto them, *"Peace be unto you."* There is peace for the conscience through His blood, and peace for the heart in His love.

Secret of Joy

Remember, then, that love is power, and peace is power; but now I will call attention to another fruit of the Spirit, and this too is power—the grace of joy. It is the privilege, I believe, of every Christian to walk in the light, as God is in the light, and to have that peace which will be flowing unceasingly as we keep busy about His work. And it is our privilege to be full of the joy of the Lord. We read, that when Philip went down to Samaria and preached, there was great joy in the city. Why? Because they believed the glad tidings. And that is the natural order, joy in believing.

When we believe the glad tidings, there comes a joy into our souls. Also we are told that our Lord sent the seventy out, and that they went forth preaching salvation in the name of Jesus Christ. The result was that there were a great many who were blessed, and the seventy returned. It says, with great joy, and when they came back they said that the very devils were subject to them, through His name. The Lord seemed to just correct them in this one thing when He said, *"Rejoice not that the devils are subject to you, but rejoice that your names are written in heaven."* There is assurance for you. They had something to rejoice in now. God doesn't ask us to rejoice over nothing, but He gives us some ground for our joy.

What would you think of man or woman who seemed very happy today and full of joy, and couldn't tell you what made them so? Suppose I should meet a man on the street, and he was so full of joy that he should get hold of both my hands and say, "Bless the Lord, I am so full of joy!" "What makes you so full of joy?" "Well, I don't know." "You don't know?" "No, I don't; but I am so joyful that I just want to get out of the flesh." Would we not think such a person unreasonable? But there are a great many people who feel—who want to feel—that they are Christians before they are Christians. They want the Christian's experience before they become Christians; they want to have the joy of the Lord before they receive Jesus Christ. But this is not the Gospel order. He brings joy when He comes, and we cannot have joy apart from Him. There is no joy away from Him. He is the author of it, and we find our joy in Him.

Joy is Unselfish

Now, there are three kinds of joy. There is the joy of one's own salvation. I thought, when I first tasted that, it was the most delicious joy I had ever known, and that I could never get beyond it. But I found, afterward, there was something more joyful that, namely, the joy of the salvation of others.

Oh, the privilege, the blessed privilege, to be used of God to win a soul to Christ, and see a man or woman being led out of bondage by some act of ours toward them. To think that God should condescend to allow us to be co-workers with Him; it is the highest honor we can wear. It surpasses the joy of our own salvation, this joy of seeing others saved. And then John said, He had no greater joy than to see His disciples walking in the truth.

Every man who has been the means of leading souls to Christ understands what that means. Young disciples, walk in the truth and you will have joy all the while.

I think there is a difference between happiness and joy. Happiness is caused by things which happen around me, and circumstances will mar it, but joy flows right on through trouble; joy flows on through the dark; joy flows in the night as well as in the day; joy flows all through persecution and opposition; if flows right along, for it is an unceasing fountain bubbling up in the heart; a secret spring which the world can't see and don't know anything about; but the Lord gives His people perpetual joy when they walk in obedience to Him.

This joy is fed by the Divine Word. Jeremiah say in chapter 15:16:

"Your words were found, and I did eat them; and your word was unto me the joy and rejoicing of my heart: for I am called by your name, O Lord."

He ate the words, and what was the result? He said they were the joy and rejoicing of his heart. Now people should look for joy in the Word, and not in the world. They should look for the joy which the Scriptures furnish, and then go work in the vineyard; because a joy that don't send me out to some one else, a joy that doesn't impel me to go and help the poor drunkard, a joy that doesn't prompt me to visit the widow and the fatherless, a joy that doesn't cause me to go into the Mission Sunday-School or other Christian work, is not worth having, and is not from above. A joy that does not constrain me to go and work for the Master is purely sentiment and not real joy.

Joy in Persecution

Then it says in Luke 6:22:

"Blessed are you, when men shall hate you, and when they shall separate you from their company, and shall reproach you, and cast out your name as evil, for the Son of man's sake. Rejoice in that day, and leap for joy: for, behold, your reward is great in heaven: for in the like manner did their fathers unto the prophets."

Christians do not receive their reward down here. We have to go right against the current of the world. We may be unpopular, and we may go right against many of our personal friends if we live godly in Christ Jesus; and at the same time, if we are persecuted for the Master's sake, we will have this joy bubbling up; it just comes right up in our hearts all the while—a joy that is unceasing—that flows right on. The world cannot choke that fountain. If we have Christ in the heart, by and by the reward will come.

The longer I live the more I am convinced that godly men and women are not appreciated in our day. But their work will live after them, and there will be a greater work done after they are gone, by the influence of their lives, than when they were living. Daniel is doing a thousand times more than when he was living in Babylon. Abraham is doing more today than he did on the plain with his tent and altar. All these centuries he has been living, and so we read:

"Blessed are the dead that die in the Lord, from henceforth; says the Spirit, that they may rest from their labors, and their works do follow them."

Let us set the streams running that shall flow on after we have gone. If we have today persecution and opposition, let us press forward, and our reward will be great by and by.

Oh! think of this; the Lord Jesus, the Maker of heaven and earth, who created the world, says, *"Great shall be thy reward."* He calls it great. If some friend should say it is great, it might be very small; but when the Lord, the great and mighty God, says it is great, what must it be? Oh, the reward that is in store for those who serve Him! We have this joy, if we serve Him. A man or woman is not fit to work for God who is cast down, because they go about their work with a sad face. *"The joy of the Lord is your strength."* What we need today is a joyful church. A joyful church will make inroads upon the works of Satan, and we will see the Gospel going down into dark lanes and dark alleys, and into dark garrets and cellars, and we will see the drunkards reached and the gamblers and the harlots come pressing into the Kingdom of God. It is this carrying a sad countenance, with so many wrinkles on our brows, which retards Christianity. Oh may there come great joy upon believers everywhere, and that we may shout for joy and rejoice in God day and night. A joyful church—let us pray for that, that the Lord may make us joyful, and when we have joy then we will have success. If we don't have the reward we think we should have here, let us constantly remember the rewarding time will come hereafter.

Someone has said, if you had asked men in Abraham's day who their great man was, they would have said Enoch or Abraham. If you had asked in Moses' day who their great man was, they would not have said it was Moses; he was nothing, but it would have been Abraham. If you had asked in the days of Elijah or Daniel, it wouldn't have been Daniel of Elijah, they were nothing; but it would have been Moses. And in the days of Jesus Christ if you had asked about John the Baptist or the apostles, you would hear they were mean and contemptible in the sight of the world, and were looked upon with scorn and reproach;

but see how mighty they have become. And so we will not be appreciated in our day, but we are to toil on and work on, possessing this joy all the while.

And if we lack it, let us cry: *"Restore unto me the joy of Your salvation, and uphold me with Your free Spirit; then will I teach transgressors Your ways, and sinners shall be converted unto You."* Again, the 15th chapter of John, and 11th verse reads: *"These things have I spoken to you, that my joy might remain in you, and {that} your joy might be full."* And in the 16th chapter and 22d verse: *"And you now therefore have sorrow: but I will see you again, and your heart shall rejoice, and your joy no man takes from you.*

I am so thankful that I have a joy that the world cannot rob me of. I have a treasure that the world cannot take from me. I have something that is not in the power of man or devil to deprive me of, and that is the joy of the Lord. *"No man can take it from you."*

In the second century, they brought a martyr before a king, and the king wanted him to recant and give up Christ and Christianity, but the man spurned the proposition. So the king said; "If you don't do it, I will banish you." The man smiled and answered: "You can't banish me from Christ, for He says He will never leave me nor forsake me." The king got angry, and said: "Well, I will confiscate your property and take it all from you." Then the man replied: "My treasures are laid up on high; you cannot get them." The king became still more angry, and said: "I will kill you." "Why," the man answered, "I have been dead forty years; I have been dead with Christ, dead to the world, and my life is hid with Christ in God, and you cannot touch it."

And so we can rejoice, because we are on resurrection ground, having risen with Christ. Let persecution and opposition come, we can rejoice continually, and remember that our reward is great, reserved for us unto the day when He who is our Life shall appear, and we shall appear with Him in glory.

CHAPTER 5

Power Hindered

Israel, we are told, limited the Holy One of Israel. They vexed and grieved the Holy Spirit, and rebelled against His authority, but there is a special sin against Him, which we may profitably consider. The first description of it is in Matthew, chapter 12.

The Unpardonable Sin

"Then was brought unto him one possessed with a devil, blind, and dumb: and he healed him, insomuch that the blind and dumb both spoke and saw. And all the people were amazed, and said, 'Is not this the son of David?' But when the Pharisees heard it, they said, 'This fellow does not cast out devils, but by Beelzebub the prince of the devils.' And Jesus knew their thoughts, and said unto them, 'Every kingdom divided against itself is brought to desolation; and every city or house divided against itself shall not stand: And if Satan cast out Satan, he is divided against himself; how then shall his kingdom stand? And if I by Beelzebub cast out devils, by whom do your children cast them out?

Therefore they shall be your judges. But if I cast out devils by the Spirit of God, then the kingdom of God is come unto you. Or else how can one enter into a strong man's house, and spoil his goods, except he first bind the strong man? And then he will spoil his house. He that is not with me is against me; and he that gathers not with me scatters abroad. Therefore I say to you, All manner of sin and blasphemy shall be forgiven unto men: but the blasphemy against the Holy Ghost shall not be forgiven unto men. And whosoever speaks a word against the Son of man, it shall be forgiven him: but whosoever speaks against the Holy Ghost, it shall not be forgiven him, neither in this world, neither in the world to come.'"

That is Matthew's account. Now let us read Mark's account in chapter 3:21:

"And when His friends heard of it, they went out to lay hold of Him, for they said: 'He (that is Christ) is beside Himself. And the scribes which came down from Jerusalem said, He hath Beelzebub, and by the prince of the devils casts He out devils.'" The word *Beelzebub means the Lord of Filth. They charged the Lord Jesus with being possessed not only with an evil spirit, but with a filthy spirit.*

"And He called them unto Him, and said unto them in parables, 'How can Satan cast out Satan? And if a kingdom is divided against itself, that kingdom cannot stand. And if a house is divided against itself, that house cannot stand. And if Satan rises up against himself, and be divided, he cannot stand, but has an end. No man can enter into a strong

man's house, and spoil his goods, except he will first bind the strong man; and then he will spoil his house. Truly I say to you, all sins shall be forgiven the sons of men, and blasphemies by which they shall blaspheme: but he that shall blaspheme against the Holy Ghost has not forgiveness, but is in danger of eternal damnation.'"

Now, if it stopped there, we would be left perhaps in darkness, and we would not exactly understand what the sin against the Holy Ghost is. But the next verse of this same chapter of Mark just throws light upon the whole matter, and we need not be in darkness another minute if we really want light; for observe, the verse reads: *"Because they said, 'He has and unclean spirit.'"*

Now, I have met a good many atheists and skeptics and deists and infidels, both in this country and abroad, but I never in my life met a man or woman who ever said that Jesus Christ was possessed of an unclean devil. Did you? I don't think you every met such a person. I have heard men say bitter things against Christ, but I never heard any man stand up and say that he thought Jesus Christ was possessed with the devil, and that he cast out devils by the power of the devil. I don't believe any man or woman has any right to say they have committed the unpardonable sin, unless they have maliciously, and willfully and deliberately said that they believe that Jesus Christ had a devil in Him, and that He was under the power of the devil, and that He cast out devils by the power of the devil. Because you perhaps have heard someone say that there is such a thing as grieving the Spirit of God, and resisting the Spirit of God until he has taken His flight and left you, then you have said, "That is the unpardonable sin."

What it is Not

I admit there is such a thing as resisting the Spirit of God, and resisting till the Spirit of God has departed. But if the Spirit of God has left any, they will not be troubled about their sins. The very fact that they are troubled, shows that the Spirit of God has not left them. If a man is troubled about his sins, it is the work of the Spirit. For Satan never yet told him he was a sinner. Satan makes us believe that we are pretty good; that we are good enough without God, safe without Christ and that we don't need salvation. But when a man wakes up to the fact that he is lost, that he is a sinner, that is the work of the Spirit. If the Spirit of God had left him, he would not be in that state; and because men and women want to be Christians, is a sign that the Spirit of God is drawing them.

If resisting the Spirit of God is an unpardonable sin, then we have all committed it, and there is no hope for any of us. I do not believe there is a minister, or a worker in Christ's vineyard, who has not, some time in his life, resisted the Holy Ghost; who has not some time in his life rejected the Spirit of God. To resist the Holy Ghost is one thing, and to commit that awful sin of blasphemy against the Holy Ghost, is another thing. Let us take the Scripture and just compare them. Now, some people say, "I have such blasphemous thoughts; there are some awful thoughts that come into my mind against God," and they think that is the unpardonable sin. We are not to blame for having ...

When bad thoughts come into our minds we are not to harbor them, then we are to blame. But if the devil comes and darts an evil thought into my mind, and I say, "Lord help me," sin is not reckoned to me. Who has not had evil thoughts come into his mind, flash into his heart, and been called to fight them? One old divine says, "You are not to blame for the birds that fly over your head, but if you allow them to come down and make a nest in your hair, then you are to blame. You are to blame if you don't fight them off."

And so with these evil thoughts that come flashing into our minds, we have to fight them. We are not to harbor them, nor to entertain them. If I have evil thoughts and desires come into my mind, it is no sign that I have committed the unpardonable sin. If I love these thoughts and harbor them, and think evil of God, and think Jesus Christ a blasphemer, I am responsible for such gross iniquity. But if I charge Him with being the prince of devils, then I am committing the unpardonable sin.

The Faithful Friend

Let us now consider the sin of "Grieving the Spirit." Resisting the Holy Ghost is one thing, grieving Him is another. Stephen charged the unbelieving Jews in the 7th chapter of Acts, *"You always resist the Holy Ghost as your fathers did."* The world has always been resisting the Spirit of God in all ages. That is the history of the world. The world is today resisting the Holy Spirit.

"Faithful are the wounds of a friend." The Divine Spirit as a friend reveals to this poor world its faults and the world only hates Him for it. He shows them the plague of their hearts. He convinces or convicts them of sin, therefore they fight the spirit of God. I believe there is

many a man resisting the Holy Ghost. I believe there is many a man today fighting against the Spirit of God.

In the 4th chapter of Ephesians, in the 30th, 31st, and 32d verses, we read:

"And grieve not the holy Spirit of God, whereby you are sealed unto the day of redemption. Let all bitterness, and wrath, and anger, and clamor, and evil speaking, be put away from you, with all malice: And be kind one to another, tenderhearted, forgiving one another, even as God for Christ's sake has forgiven you."

Now, mark you, that was written to the Church at Ephesus. *"Grieve not the Holy Spirit, whereby you are sealed unto the day of redemption."* I believe today that Churches all of over Christendom are guilty of grieving the Holy Spirit. There are a good many believers in different churches wondering why the work of God is not revived.

The Church Grieves the Spirit

I think that if we search, we will find something in the Church grieving the Spirit of God. It may be a mere schism in the church; it may be some unsound doctrine; or it may be some division in the Church. There is one thing I have noticed as I have traveled in different countries; I never yet have known the Spirit of God to work where the Lord's people were divided. There is one thing that we must have if we are to have the Holy Spirit of God to work in our midst, and that is unity. If a church is divided, the members should immediately seek unity. Let the believers come together and get the difficulty out of the way. If the minister of a church cannot unite the people, if those that were dissatisfied will not fall in, it would be better for that minister to retire. I think there are a good many ministers in this country who are losing their time; they have lost, some of them, months and years; they have not seen any fruit, and they will not see any fruit, because they have a divided church. Such a church cannot grow in divine things. The Spirit of God doesn't work were there is division, and what we want today is the spirit of unity among God's children, so that the Lord may work.

Worldly Amusements

Then, another thing, I think, that grieves the Spirit, is the miserable policy of introducing questionable entertainments. There are lotteries, for instance, that we have in many churches. If a man wants to gamble, he doesn't have to go to some gambling den; he can stay in the church. And there are fairs—bazaars, as they call them—where they have raffles and grab-bags. And if he wants to see a drama, he doesn't need to go to the theater, for many of our churches are turned into theaters. He may stay right in the church and witness the acting. I believe all these things grieve the Spirit of God. I believe when we bring the Church down to the level of the world to reach the world, we are losing all the while and grieving the Spirit of God. But some say, if we take that standard and lift it up high, it will drive away a great many members from our churches. I believe it, and I think the quicker they are gone the better. The world has come into the Church like a flood, and how often you find an ungodly choir employed to do the singing for the whole congregation. How do we get the idea that we need an ungodly man to sing praises to God! It was not long ago I heard of a church where they had an unconverted choir, and the minister saw something about the choir that he didn't like, and he spoke to the choirmaster, but the choirmaster replied: "You attend to your end of the church, and I will attend to mine." You cannot expect the Spirit of God to work in a church in such a state as that.

Unconverted Choirs

Paul tells us not to speak in an unknown tongue, and if we have choirs who are singing in an unknown tongue, why is not that just as great an abomination? I have been in churches where they have had a choir, who would rise and sing, and sing, and it seemed as if they sung five or ten minutes, and I could not understand one solitary word they sung, and all the while the people were looking around carelessly. There are, perhaps, a select few, very fond of fine music, and they want to bring the opera right into the church, and so they have opera music in the church, and the people, who are drowsy and sleepy, don't take part in the singing. They hire ungodly men, unconverted men, and these men will sometimes get the Sunday paper, and get back in the organ loft, and the moment the minister begins his sermon, they will take out their papers and read them all the while that the minister is preaching. The organist, provided he does not go out for a walk if he happens to keep awake, will read his paper, or perhaps, a novel, while the minister is preaching. And the minister wonders why God doesn't revive His work. He wonders why he is losing his hold on the congregation. He wonders why people don't come crowding into the church; why people are running after the world instead of coming into the church. The trouble is that we have let down the standard. We have grieved the Spirit of God. One movement of God's power is worth more than all our artificial power, and what the Church of God wants today is to get down in the dust of humiliation and confession of sin, and go out and be separated from the world; and then see if we do not have power with God and with man.

What is Success?

The Gospel has not lost its power; it is just as powerful today as it ever has been. We don't want any new doctrine. It is still the old Gospel with the old power, the Holy Ghost power. And if the churches will but confess their sins and put them away, and lift the standard instead of pulling it down, and pray to God to lift us all up into a higher and holier life, then the fear of the Lord will come upon the people around us.

It was when Jacob put away strange gods and set his face toward Bethel that the fear of God fell upon the nations around. And when the churches turn towards God, and we cease grieving the Spirit, so that He may work through us, we will then have conversions all the while. Believers will be added to the Church daily. It is sad when you look over Christendom and see how desolate it is, and see how little spiritual life, spiritual power, there is in the Church of God today, many of the church members not even wanting this Holy Ghost power. They don't desire it; they want intellectual power; they want to get some man who will just draw; and a choir that will draw; not caring whether anyone is saved. With them that is not the question. Only fill the pews, have good society, fashionable people, and dancing. Such persons are found one night at the theater and the next night at the opera. They don't like the prayer-meetings; but instead they abominate them. If the minister will only lecture and entertain, that would suit them.

I said to a man some time ago, "How are you getting on at your Church?" Oh, splendid. "Many conversions?" "Well, well, on that side we are not getting on so well. But," he said, "we rented all our pews and are able to pay all our running expenses; we are getting on splendidly." That is what the godless call "getting on splendidly;" because they rent the pews, pay the minister, and pay the running expenses. Conversions! That is a strange thing.

There was a man being shown through one of the cathedrals of Europe. He had come in from the country, and one of the men belonging to the cathedral was showing him around, when he inquired, "Do you have many conversions here?" "Many what?" "Many conversions here?" "Ah, man, this is not a Wesleyan chapel." The idea of there being conversions there! And you can go into a good many churches in this country and ask if they have many conversions there, and they would not know what it meant, they are so far away from the Lord; they are not looking for conversions, and don't expect them.

Shipwrecks

Alas! See how many young converts have made shipwreck against such churches. Instead of being a harbor of delight to them, they have proved false lights, alluring them to destruction. Isn't it time for us to get down on our faces before God and cry mightily to Him to forgive us our sins. The quicker we own it the better. You may be invited to a party, and it may be made up of church members, and what will be the conversation? Oh, I got so sick of such parties that I left years ago. I would not think of spending a night that way; it is a waste of time; there is hardly a chance to say a word for the Master. If you talk of a personal Christ, your company becomes offensive; they don't like it; they want you to talk about the world, about a popular minister, a popular church, a good organ, a good choir, and they say, "Oh, we have a grand organ, and a superb choir," and all that, and it suits them; but that doesn't warm the Christian heart. When you speak of a risen Christ and a personal Savior, they don't like it.

The fact is, the world has come into the church and taken possession of it, and what we want to do is to wake up and ask God to forgive us for "Grieving the Spirit." Dear reader, search your heart and inquire. Have I done anything to grieve the Spirit of God? If you have, may God show it to you today. If you have done any thing to grieve the Spirit of God, you want to know it today, and get down on your face before God and ask Him to forgive you and help you to put it away. I have lived long enough to know that if I cannot have the power of the Spirit of God on me to help me to work for Him. I would rather die, than live just for the sake of living. How many are there in the church today who have been members for fifteen or twenty years, but have never done a solitary thing for Jesus Christ? They cannot lay their hands upon one solitary soul who has been blessed through their influence. They cannot point today to one single person who has ever been lifted up by them.

Quench Not

In 1st Thessalonians, 5th chapter, we are told not to Quench the Spirit. Now, I am confident the cares of the world are coming in and quenching the Spirit with a great many. They say: "I don't care for the world." O perhaps not the pleasures of the world so much after all as the cares of this life; but they have just let the cares come in and quench the Spirit of God. Anything that comes between me and God—between my soul and God—quenches the Spirit. It may be my family. You may say: "Is there any danger of loving my family too much?" Not if we love God more; but God must have the first place. If I love my family more than God, then I am quenching the Spirit of God within me. If I love wealth, if I love fame, if I love honor, if I love position, if I love pleasure, if I love self, more than I love God who created and saved me, then I am committing a sin. I am not only grieving the Spirit of God, but quenching Him, and robbing my soul of His power.

Emblems of the Spirit

But I would further call attention to the emblems of the Holy Spirit. An emblem is something that represents an object. The same as a balance is an emblem of justice, and a crown and emblem of royalty, and a scepter is an emblem of power. So we find in the 17th chapter of Exodus and 6th verse, that water is an emblem of the Holy Spirit. You find in the Smitten Rock, in the wilderness, the work of the Trinity illustrated.

"Behold, I will stand before you there upon the rock in Horeb; and you shall smite the rock, and there shall come water out of it, that the people may drink." And Moses did so in the sight of the elders of Israel.

Paul declares, in Corinthians, that the rock was Christ—it represented Christ. God says: *"I will stand upon the rock,"* and as Moses smote the rock the water came out, which was an emblem of the Holy Spirit; and it flowed out along through the camp; and they drank of the water.

Now water is cleansing; it is fertilizing; it is refreshing; it is abundant, and it is freely given. And so the Spirit of God is the same: cleansing, fertilizing, refreshing, reviving, and He was freely given when the smitten Christ was glorified.

Then, too, fire is an emblem of the Spirit; it is purifying, illuminating, searching. We talk about searching our hearts. We cannot do it. What we want is to have God search them. O that God may search us and bring out the hidden things, the secret things that cluster there and bring them to light.

The wind is another emblem. It is independent, powerful, sensible in its effects, and reviving; how the Spirit of God revives when He comes to all the drooping members of the Church. Then the rain and the dew—fertilizing, refreshing, abundant; and the dove, gentle—what more gentle than the dove; and the lamb?—gentle, meek, and innocent sacrifice. We read of the wrath of God. We read of the wrath of the Lamb, but nowhere do we read of the wrath of the Holy Spirit—gentle, innocent, meek, loving; and that Spirit wants to take possession of our hearts. And He comes as a voice, another emblem—speaking, guiding, warning, teaching; and the seal—impressing, securing, and making us as His own.

May we know Him in all His wealth of blessing. This is my prayer for myself and for you. May we heed the words of the great Apostle:

> "My speech and my preaching was not with enticing words of man's wisdom, but in demonstration of the Spirit, and of power: that your faith should not stand in the wisdom of men, but in the power of God."

Gems

from D. L. Moody

One thing I have noticed in studying the Word of God, and that is, when a man is filled with the Spirit he deals largely with the Word of God, whereas the man who is filled with his own ideas refers rarely to the Word of God. He gets along without it, and you seldom see it mentioned in his discourses.

———•◆•———

When the Spirit came to Moses, the plagues came upon Egypt and he had power to destroy men's lives. When the Spirit came upon Elijah, fire came down from heaven. When the Spirit came upon Gideon, no man could stand before him. And when the Spirit came upon Joshua, he marched around the city of Jericho and the whole city fell into his hands. But when the Spirit came upon the Son of Man, He gave his life and healed the broken-hearted.

———•◆•———

Another thing the Spirit of God does is to give liberty. Where the Spirit is, there is liberty. In a good deal of our church work there is almost everything but liberty. A good deal of our work is forced work. Sometimes it takes a good deal of strength to get out a work. Why? Because the atmosphere is not right. The Holy Spirit must have the right atmosphere to work in. You take the atmosphere out of this room and my voice wouldn't be heard three feet away from me. You have got to have air to convey sound, and you have got to have the Spirit prepare the ground in order to carry home the truth. If you get into a certain atmosphere where the Spirit isn't working you will not have liberty.

———•◦•———

If a minister doesn't have liberty, it isn't always his fault. I want to emphasize that. The fault may be down there in the audience.

———•◦•———

It is well for us to remember that the Holy Spirit is a person.

———•◦•———

First, there must be a willing mind and heart; we must know the mind of the Holy Spirit, give ourselves up wholly to be led and guided and filled with the Spirit.

———•◦•———

It seems to me that the first impulse, the first aim, of a new-born soul is service. "What shall I do? I want to do something." This desire is out of gratitude to Him who has saved you.

———•◦•———

When Christ had finished His work the last thing He did was to teach His disciples about the coming of the Holy Spirit and what He would do when He came. When

He handed over His work to them, then it was He told them that the Spirit was coming to help and to work with them. It was this that helped those early Christians, and it will help us. There is not a man or woman here today who may not be helped if he will.

———•·•·•———

I have in mind a minister who said, "I have heart disease, I can't preach more than once a week," so he had a colleague preach for him once a week and do the visiting. He was an old minister and couldn't do any visiting. He had heard o the anointing of power, and he said, "I would like to be anointed for my burial. I would like before I go hence to preach once with power." He prayed that God would fill him with the Spirit, and I met him not long after that, and he said, "I have preached on an average eight times a week, and have seen conversions all along." The Spirit came on him. I don't believe that man broke down at first due to hard work, so much as using the machinery without oil, without lubrication. It is not the hard work that breaks down ministers, but it is the toil of working without power. Oh, that God may anoint His people! Not the ministry only, but every disciple.

———•·•·•———

If you have no desire, no longing, for usefulness, I would say there is something wrong with your life.

———•·•·•———

It is God's work to carry home conviction to the heart, not man's work.

A great many people are trying to make themselves love God. You cannot do it. Love must be spontaneous. You cannot love by trying to make yourself love. When the heart has been filled with the Spirit of God you cannot help loving Him. But you cannot make yourself love. More love is just what we want today! If you should ask me what the church needs, I would say "love."

———————

If we have a praise church we will have people converted.

———————

I wish we could get this accursed spirit of criticism out of the church, and then there would be something done.

———————

You go into some churches and you will find some men that are very dry, and a man right next to him with a sunny face, and there all is fresh and bright. Why? Because one has the anointing, has the blessing; and the other sits there where the rain is pouring down, and doesn't get under it at all. Let's get under the pierced clouds, and then just keep the heart full.

———————

When the Spirit of God is in a man, the fire just burns. But thank God, although Samson lost his strength, it came back to him. And some of you Samsons that have lost your power can get it back again if you will. God used Peter far more after He restored him than He did before his fall.

Praise is not only speaking to the Lord on our own account, but it is praising Him for what He has done for others.

━━━━━•◦•━━━━━

John and Peter were filled in the second chapter of Acts, and again in the fourth. Now, they had either lost some of their power, or had greater capacity. If Peter and John needed to be filled again so soon after Pentecost, don't you think you and I need to be filled again?

━━━━━•◦•━━━━━

When a man is full of the love of God, he has power to resist temptation. When the heart is filled with the Holy Spirit, and Satan comes to put in an evil thought, he throws off the temptation.

━━━━━•◦•━━━━━

There is joy in the service of Christ that the world knows nothing of, and you never will until you taste it.

━━━━━•◦•━━━━━

My friends, God never makes a mistake; and if when He looks down into your hearts and sees truth there, He will forgive you. You will have liberty to walk and talk with and work for Christ if you have His Spirit.

━━━━━•◦•━━━━━

We shall draw the world to Christ when we are filled with religion.

What can botanists tell you of the lily of the valley? You must study this book for that. What can geologists tell you of the Rock of Ages, or mere astronomers about the Bright Morning Star? In these pages we find all knowledge unto salvation; here we read of the ruin of man by nature, redemption by the blood, and regeneration by the Holy Ghost. These three things run all through and through them.

———◆●◆———

It is the greatest pleasure of living to win souls to Christ.

———◆●◆———

If you are under the power of evil, and you want to get under the power of God, cry to Him to bring you over to His service; cry to Him to take you into His army. He will hear you; He will come to you, and, if need be, He will send a legion of angels to help you to fight your way up to heaven. God will take you by the right hand and lead you through this wilderness, over death, and take you right into His kingdom. That's what the Son of Man came to do. He has never deceived us; just say here; "Christ is my deliverer."

———◆●◆———

Lift your eyes from off these puny Christians—from off these human ministers, and look to Christ. He is the Savior of the world. He came from the throne to this earth: He came from the very bosom of the Father. God gave Him up freely for us, and all we have to do is to accept him as our Savior Look at Him at Gethsemane, sweating as it were great drops of blood; look at Him on the cross, crucified between two thieves; hear that piercing cry, "Father, Father, forgive them, they know not what they do." And as you look into that face, as you look into those wounds on His feet or His hands, will you say He has not the power to save you? Will you say He has not the power so redeem you?

Prayers of Moody

O ur Heavenly Father, we praise thee for Thy blessed Word. We thank thee that Thy Son didst formerly come down into this world; that He did so use his mighty power while on earth that he has power over devils and unclean spirits; that He can by a word cast out devils, and that He can save our sons and daughters, can save our children, can save our unsaved friends. O God, increase our faith today! O God, we pray that thou wilt come down upon us with the power of Thy word, and that we may have, strong faith in thee and Thy promises. We pray thee that if any evil influence, or if our sins keep back the great and mighty blessing that we want in our lives, we pray that thou wilt bring it to light. We pray that the Holy Spirit may reveal to each one of us all our sins, that we may turn away from them and hate them with a perfect hatred; that Thy Spirit may came with power upon our hearts and fill them with holy desires. O God, we pray thee that Thy blessing may rest on all the churches, upon this day of fasting and prayer. We pray that Thy blessing may rest on all the fathers and mothers in prayer with thee today, as they pour out their hearts for their children. O God, hear and answer their prayer, and may the joyful tidings of souls redeemed be coming in from all over before long. Let the summons of grace be everywhere heard, that the wilderness may blossom and the solitary places be made glad. O God, we pray thee that the churches may be blest, that the mothers, heartbroken on account of their children, may be comforted, and may those who were in darkness see the blessed light of the sun. O God, come in power upon us, and pass through our land, that a cry may be raised hear —"Jesus of Nazareth passeth by." God, hear our supplications here today and answer our prayers; answer the many prayers that are going up to thee. Come, Holy Spirit, in Thy mighty power, and convict our hearts of sin, and melt them and turn them from darkness to light. Amen.

O ur Heavenly Father, we thank thee for sending Christ into this world to seek and save that, which was lost. O Son of God! We thank thee that thou didst come for us, and thou hast laid down Thy life for the sheep, Now we pray, O God, that every lost soul in this building may come home tonight; may they no longer reject the Lord of all grace; may they no longer reject him who came to seek and to save them. Help them this night, while they are trying to receive Christ in their hearts. May this be the hour and this the night they may be brought unto salvation. We pray that Thy blessing may rest upon the words spoken in such weakness. We pray that the Spirit of the Lord may carry them home in power; that there may be many rise up and be drawn to God by these meetings; and that the Spirit of the Lord may be poured out tonight without measure upon us. We pray that the Holy Spirit may touch every heart here tonight with a sense of their true condition, that they may no longer be blinded by sin, but that their eyes may be opened; that the blessed Savior, in all His glory and loveliness, they may this night see, led by the gift of faith, standing with outstretched arms knocking at the door of their hearts, and saying, "Open, and I will come in."

May the Spirit of God speak to every heart here tonight. O Son of God, do thou speak! May there be many of the lost who shall be found tonight. By the power of the Highest, may they be saved! Then when the voice of man shall be hushed, may the gentle, mild voice of Jesus be heard saying: "Behold, I stand at the door and knock. If any man will, let him hear my voice and open the door and I will come in and sup with him and he with me." O Son of God, knock at the door of the hearts of the unsaved here tonight. May they hear that mild, gentle knocking. May they hear that heavenly voice, and may they open the door just now, and see and welcome, thrice welcome, the Son of God in their hearts. O Spirit of the living God, come upon this assembly; give us one touch from heaven just now. May the dead live; may the lost be found, and may the wanderers return home. May the Spirit of the Lord God be with us, and may many believe on the Lord God, this night, and be saved; and Christ shall have the praise and the glory. Amen.

Our Heavenly Father, we pray that Thy blessing may rest upon all that have assembled in this hall at this hour; and that every man in this assembly that is without God and without hope in this dark world may be convicted of his sin at this hour. We pray that the Holy Ghost may do his work; and that there may be many that shall look back, in after years, to this hour and this hall, as the time and place where they became children of God and heirs of eternal life. We pray that thou wilt bless them; and wilt thou bless the gospel that shall be spoken this afternoon, and may it reach many hearts. May there be many led by the Spirit of God, this day, to the cross of Christ, there to cast their burden and their guilt upon him who came into the world to put away the sins of the world by the sacrifice of himself. And may there be many here who shall hear the loving voice of the Good Shepherd saying unto them, "Come unto me all ye that are burdened and heavy laden, and I will give you rest;" and may those that are burdened and heavy laden find rest in Christ today May those that are cast down on account of their sins, this day be lifted up by the gospel of Jesus Christ. And, O God, we pray thee that thou wouldst snap the fetters that bind them and set the poor bondsmen free today; and may this be the day that they shall come unto thee. And Thy name shall have the power and the glory forever. Amen.

Christ Our All in All

*"Where there is neither Greek nor Jew,
circumcision nor uncircumcision, Barbarian,
Scythian, bond nor free: but Christ is all,
and in all"* (Colossians 3:11).

CHRIST is all in all to every one who has truly found Him. He is our Savior, Redeemer, Deliverer, Shepherd, Teacher, and also sustains toward us many more offices, to which I desire to call your attention.

1. Christ is our SAVIOR

If we turn to Luke 2:10, 11, we find Christ is there announced as our SAVIOR: "Behold, I bring you good tidings of great joy, which shall be to all people. For unto you is born this day in the city of David a Savior, which is Christ the Lord."

We learn to know Christ as our Savior, to meet Him on Mount Calvary, to look on Him as the bleeding Lamb of God, before we know Him as our Redeemer, Deliverer, and Shepherd. Now, looking round upon this vast assembly, I, who do not know the hearts of the people, cannot know whether you can say that Christ is your Savior. There are many, I trust, who can say this, and who rejoice in His salvation; while, without being uncharitable, I am afraid there are many who know nothing personally of Jesus as their Savior.

He is offered to every one of you today as a Savior; "God gave Him up freely for us all," that we all through Him might be saved. If you are belonging to this world, I can prove that you have a Savior. If you belonged to some other planet, such as the moon or any of the stars, then I could not say a Savior was offered to you; for it is not revealed whether the people of these distant worlds, even if they are inhabited, require salvation or not. But this I know, that every man on this globe has a Savior offered him.

Salvation Free To All

I have no sympathy with those men who try to limit God's salvation to a certain few. I believe that Christ died for all who will come. I have received many letters finding fault with me, and saying I surely don't believe the doctrine of election. I do believe in election; but I have no business to preach that doctrine to the world at large. The world has nothing to do with election; it has only to do with the invitation, "Whosoever will, let him take the water of life freely." That is the message for the sinner. I am sent to preach the gospel to all.

After you have received salvation, we can talk about election. It's a doctrine for Christians, for the Church, not for the unconverted world. Our message is "good tidings, which shall be to all people; for unto you is born this day a Savior, which is Christ the Lord." All people, this Savior is proffered to you. Accept Him, and God will accept you; reject Him, and God will reject you. Your eternal destiny depends on your refusal or otherwise to accept the proffered Savior. The case is simply one of giving and taking. God gives; I receive. We must, then, first of all know Christ as our Savior.

2. But He is still more: He is our REDEEMER.

Supposing I saw a man tumble into a river, and I were to jump in and rescue him, I would be a savior to him—I would have saved him. But when I brought the man ashore, I would probably leave him and do nothing further.

But the Lord does more. He not only saves us, but He redeems us—that is, He buys us back. He ransoms us from the power of sin, as if I would promise to watch over that rescued man forever, and see that he did not again fall into the water. The Lord not only saves us from spiritual death, but He redeems us forever that death can never touch us.

Liberty to the Captives

When I was at Richmond, Virginia, the African people were going to have a meeting. It was the first day of their freedom. I went to their church, and never before or since heard such bursts of eloquence.

"Mother," said one, "rejoice today. Your little child has been sold from you for the last time; your posterity is forever free. Glory to God in the highest! Young men, you have heard the driver's whip for the last time; you are free today! Young maidens, you have been put up on the auction-block for the last time!" They spoke right out, they shouted for joy; their prayers had been answered, and it was the gospel to them. In like manner Jesus Christ proclaims liberty to the captives. Some have accepted it; some, like the poor slaves, scarcely believe the good tidings;

but it is nonetheless true. Christ has come to redeem us from the slavery of sin.

Now, who will accept of that redemption? There was one black woman, a servant in an inn in the Southern States, who could not believe she was free. "Am I free, or not?" she asked of a visitor. Her master told her she was not, but her brethren told her she was. For two years she had been free without knowing it. She represents a great many in the Church of God today. They can have liberty, and yet they don't know it.

3. Again, Christ is our DELIVERER.

The children of Israel were not only saved and redeemed from the bondage of the Egyptians, but they were also delivered, that they should not be led back again into bondage. Many are afraid; they think they are not able to hold on, and therefore shrink from making a profession. But Christ is able to keep you from falling. He is able to deliver you in the dark hour of trial and temptation, from every evil device of Satan, and from the snare of the fowler.

In Isaiah 49:24, we read: "Shall the prey be taken from the mighty, or the lawful captive delivered? But so says the Lord, Even the captives of the mighty shall be taken away, and the prey of the terrible shall be delivered: for I will contend with him that contends with you, and I will save your children." I will save him; I will deliver him. The children of Israel were saved from the cruel bondage of Egypt, they were led out of the land of Goshen; but still they were not fully delivered. The great host of the Egyptians was thundering behind them. It was not till they had passed

194

safely through the Red Sea, which closing behind, them, swallowed up the host of the enemy—it was not till then that they were free, that they were delivered.

Similarly in our times of danger we shall find it to be true of Christ, "He delivered my soul." And again in Job 33:24, "Then He is gracious unto him, and says, 'Deliver him from going down to the pit: I have found a ransom. His flesh shall be fresher than a child's: he shall return to the days of his youth: he shall pray unto God, and He will be favorable unto him: and he shall see His face with joy: for He will render unto man His righteousness. He will deliver his soul from going into the pit, and his life shall see the light.'" Here we have the saving, the redeeming, the deliverance from the pit. Man is fallen into the deep pit; he is kept there a lawful captive by one who is mighty. If he is to be brought back from the darkness of the pit to see the light, then we must have a ransom. Here God comes forward, and says, "I have found a ransom." Christ is the ransom, and He will deliver us. Sound out the cry, "Christ is our deliverer!" He is mighty to save, He is able to deliver.

4. Christ is A LEADER

But now we need something more. Look back again to the children of Israel. When they had marched gloriously through the Red Sea, they had been saved, redeemed, and delivered; but was that all they required? No, they had been brought into the wilderness. What now do they need? They must have a way to go in the pathless desert. They required a leader. Then Christ is the way and the leader. Are we in difficulties, in doubt, or in perplexity? Christ is our way. "I am the way, the truth, and the life" (John 10).

I have heard some say, "Well, if I am converted, and become religious, I don't know what church I would go to. There are so many different churches and denominations. I really don't know which is the right one." Hence some people are bewildered, and do not know which is the true way. Well, I would say to such, Look only to Him who says, "I AM THE WAY." He is the only true way, and if you want to reach the kingdom you have only to follow Him. We may be in darkness, but He is able to lead us in the right path. He is the Shepherd of His flock. He will go before us and lead us. He is calling upon us to arise and follow Him, and He will lead us by a way we know not. He will guide us to the green pastures if we only look to Him.

The Pillar of Cloud
All that the children of Israel had to do was to follow the cloud. If the cloud rested, they rested; if the cloud moved forward, then they moved. I can imagine that the first thing Moses did, when the gray dawn of morning broke, was to look up and see if the cloud was still over the camp. By night it was a pillar of fire, lighting up the camp, and filling them with a sense of God's protecting care; by day it was a cloud shielding them from the fierce heat of the sun's rays, and sheltering them from the sight of their enemies.

Israel's Shepherd could lead them through the pathless desert. Why? Because He made it. He knew every grain of sand in it. They could not have a better leader through the wilderness than its Creator.

And, sinner, can you, in all your difficulties or doubts and fears, have a better leader than Jehovah? Oh, I do like that good old hymn:

Guide me, O Thou great Jehovah,
Pilgrim through this barren land;
I am weak, but Thou art mighty,
Hold me with Thy powerful hand.
Bread of heaven, Feed me till I want no more.

Yes, that is the true prayer of the bewildered sinner. God is able, and still more, He is willing, to lead us, and to feed us.

"You gave them bread from heaven for their hunger, and brought forth water for them out of the rock for their thirst" (Nehemiah 9:15).

He is still as able to lead any of us as He was four thousand years ago to lead the children of Israel, "For I am the Lord; I change not." To every one of us He says, "Fear not, I will lead you; I will help you." Wonderful thing, is it not, to have God to help us on our way? In our Western countries, when men go out hunting into the dense backwoods, where there are no roads or paths of any kind, they take their hatchet and cut a little chip out of the bark of the trees as they go along, and then they easily find their way by these "blazes." They call it "blazing the way." And so, if you will allow me the expression, Christ has "blazed the way." He has traveled the road Himself, and knowing the way, He tells us to follow Him, and He will lead us safe on high.

Now we have seen Christ is our Savior, Redeemer, Deliverer, Leader, or Way. But He is more than all that.

5. Christ is our LIGHT.

"I am the light of the world: he that follows me shall not walk in darkness, but shall have the light of life." He shall have the very "light of life." Yes, it is the privilege of every Christian to walk in an unclouded sky.

But do we walk thus in an unclouded sky? No, most Christians are often in darkness. If I were to ask this congregation if they were all walking in the light, I believe there is scarcely one, if he spoke the true feeling of his heart, but would reply, "No, I am often in darkness." Why is that? It is because we are not following Christ, and keeping close to Him. We are much in darkness when we might be in the light.

Suppose the windows of this building were all closed, and we were complaining of the darkness, what would anyone say to us? Why, they would say, "Admit the light; open the windows all round, and you'll soon have plenty of light." Similarly we must let in Christ, who is the light, and open our minds to receive Him, and we shall soon walk in light. There is a great deal of darkness at the present time, even in the hearts of God's own people. But follow Him, and then you will have plenty of light. Then Christ will show to each of us that He is "The Light;" and He will do more, He will set us on fire with His light, that we also may shine as lights in this dark world.

May God help His own people to *shine brightly*, to flash out of darkness, that men may take knowledge of us that we have been with Jesus. But remember, the world hates the light. Christ was the light of the world, and the world sought to extinguish it at Calvary. Now He has left His people to shine. "You are the light of the world."

He has left us here to shine. He means us to be "living epistles, known and read of all men." The world is certain to watch, and to read you and me. If we are inconsistent, then you may be sure the world will take occasion to stumble at us.

The world finds plenty of difficulties on the way; let us see that we Christians do not add more stumbling blocks by our un-Christlike walk.

God help us to keep our lights burning clear and brilliant! Out West a friend of mine was walking along one of the streets one dark night, and saw approaching him a man with a lantern. As he came up close to him he noticed by the bright light that the man had got no eyes. He went past, but the thought struck him, "Surely that man is blind." He turned round, and said, "My friend, are you not blind?" "Yes." "Then what have you got the lantern for?" "I carry the lantern that people may not stumble over me, of course," said the blind man. Let us take a lesson from that blind man, and hold up our light, burning with the clear radiance of heaven, that men may not stumble over us.

Objectors have said that it's all only moonshine about Christ's people being lights on the way. Well, that's just what we believe.

6. We Reflect the Light of Christ.

Just like the moonshine, our light is borrowed light. When we are living in the light of our Savior we shine with His light: somewhat like the face of Moses, which shone after he had been in the mount with God. Let us live in an atmosphere of heaven, and we cannot help shining. But whenever we get downcast and weak in faith, then we are sure to lose our light.

I remember during the American war I was in a prayer meeting. We were all very dark and gloomy. Things had been going against us for some time.

At last an old man got up, and said, "What is the matter with us, that we are downhearted and sad? It is simply our lack of faith. Moses, Joshua, and David were men strong in faith. They believed, and therefore God honored them. Whence comes our want of faith? God is not dead. He is as powerful, as willing, to help today as ever He was. Why, then, are we not full of faith in Him? It is God-dishonoring to forget that He still has power, although our armies are defeated, and all seems dark and gloomy."

Get Above the Clouds
I will tell you what happened to me some time ago when I was out West. I wanted to reach the summit of one of the Western mountains. I had been told that sunrise was very beautiful when seen from the summit. We got up to the halfway house one afternoon, where we were to rest till midnight, and then set out for the top. Soon a little party of us started with a good guide. Before a great while it began to rain, and then it became a regular storm of thunder and lightning. I thought there was little use in going on, and said to the guide, "Guess we'd better turn back; we won't see anything this morning, with all these clouds." "Oh," said the guide, "I expect we'll soon get through these clouds, and get above them, and then we'll have a glorious view." So we went on, while the thunders were rumbling right about our ears. But soon we began to get above the thundercloud; the air was quite clear, and when the sun rose we had a splendid view of his rays as they tinged the

hilltops. Then, as the glorious sunshine began to break on where we stood, we could see the dark cloud far beneath our mountain height. That's what God's people want—to get into the clear air above the stormy clouds, and to CLIMB HIGHER away up to the mountain peak. There you'll catch the first rays from the Sun of Righteousness far above the clouds and mists. Some of you may be in great darkness and gloom; but fear not, climb higher, get nearer to the Master, and soon you'll catch His bright rays on your own soul, and they will sprinkle back upon others.

Keep The Lower Lights Burning
We must live as children of the light, not as children of the darkness. If we are dark and sorrowful, how is the world to know that we are children of peace, and joy, and gladness? Our determination must be to keep our lights burning. A few years ago, at the mouth of Cleveland harbor there were two lights, one at each side of the bay, called the upper and lower lights; and, to enter the harbor safely by night, vessels must sight both of these lights.

These Western lakes are more dangerous sometimes than the great ocean.

One wild, stormy night a steamer was trying to make her way into the harbor. The captain and the pilot were anxiously watching for the lights.

By and by the pilot was heard to say, "Do you see the lower lights?" "No," was the reply; "but I fear we have passed them." "Ah, there are the lights," said the pilot; "and they must be, from the bluff on which they stand, the upper lights. We have passed the lower lights, and have lost our chance of getting into the harbor." What was to be done? They looked back, and saw the dim outline of the lower lighthouse against the sky. The lights had gone out. "Can't you turn her head around?" "No; the night is too wild for that. She won't answer her helm." The storm was so fearful that they could do nothing. They tried again to make for the harbor, but they went crashing against the rocks, and sank to the bottom. Very few escaped; the great majority found a watery grave. Why? Simply because the lower lights had gone out.

And with us the upper lights are all right. Christ Himself is the upper light, and we are the lower lights, and the cry to us is, keep the lower lights burning. That is what we have to do. In the place God has put us He expects us to shine, to be living witnesses, to be a bright and shining light.

While we are here our work is to shine for Him, and He will lead us safe to the sunlit shore of Canaan, where there is no more night.

7. Christ is Our TEACHER.

What a wonderful thing to have a teacher sent from heaven. "If any man lack wisdom, let him ask of God, that gives to all men liberally, and without reproach; and it shall be given him" (James 1:5).

"If any lack wisdom:" I am afraid there are a great many of us who lack wisdom, and even the best of us at times will be in perplexity. There are moments in the life of us all when we seem in a fix; we just stand still, and say, "What shall I do? I don't know what is the best way." Oh, leave it with God, He will Himself be our teacher! "Come unto me, all you that labor and are heavy laden, and I will give you rest. Take my yoke upon you, and learn of me." Here is a wonderful teacher. He has had a school for many thousand years; He has had the best men in His school; but there's always room for another scholar there. His college is not too full yet, and the teacher is the One sent from heaven.

Any one, every one in this assembly may join this school. Jesus will welcome you there. Are you in doubt about anything? Ask Jesus; He will tell you.

Anxious sinner, seek the good teacher, as Nicodemus did: "Master, we know your are a teacher sent from God." If you seek Him thus He will direct you. He will keep you, and lead you into green pastures and by the still waters. I met a woman the other day who was full of infidel doubts and fancies. She could not believe. Reading for some time infidel works had thrown a dark and gloomy pall over her mind. It made me sad to see her in such a case. Some of you may be like her. I wish you would take Christ as your teacher, and then all darkness would flee away.

Christ is able to teach us. See how He taught the disciples. He never wearied of their learning from Him. So He will teach us if we will only listen to Him.

The Old Judge Converted

I remember, as I was coming out of the daily prayer meeting in one of our American cities a few years ago, a lady said she wished to speak to me; her voice trembled with emotion, and I saw at once that she was heavily burdened by something or other. She said she had long been praying for her husband, and she wanted to know if I would go to see him; she thought it might do him some good. What is his name? "Judge —," and she mentioned one of the most eminent politicians in the State. "I have heard of him," I said; "I am afraid I need not go, he is a booked infidel; I cannot argue with him." "That is not what he wants," said the lady. "He has had too much argument already. Go and speak to him about his soul." I said I would, although I was not very hopeful. I went to his house, was admitted to his room, and introduced myself as having come to speak to him about salvation. "Then you have come on a very foolish errand," said he; "there's no use in attacking me, I tell you that. I am proof against all these things, I don't believe in them." Well, I saw it was no use arguing with him; so I said, "I'll pray for you, and I want you to promise me that when you are converted you'll let me know." "Oh, yes, I'll let you know," he said in a tone of sarcasm. "Oh, yes, I'll let you know when I'm converted!" I left him, but I continued to pray for him. Some time subsequently I heard that the old judge was converted. I was again preaching in that city a while after that, and when I had finished talking the judge himself came to me, and said: "I promised I'd let you know when I was converted; I have come to tell you of it. Have you not heard of it?" "Yes; but I would like to hear from you how it happened." "Well," said the judge, "one night, some time after you called on me, my wife had gone to the meeting; there was no one in the house but the servants. I sat by the drawing-room fire, and I began to think: Suppose my wife is right, that there is a heaven and a hell; and suppose she is on the right way to heaven? Where am I going? I just dismissed the thought. But a second thought came: Surely He who created me is able to teach me. Yes, I thought, that is so. Then why not ask Him? I struggled against it, but at last, though I was too proud to get down on my knees, I just said, 'Father, all is dark; You who created me can teach me.' Somehow, the more I prayed the worse I felt. I was very sad. I did not wish my wife to come home and find me this way, so I slipped away to bed, and when she came into the room I pretended to be asleep. She got down on her knees and prayed. I knew she was praying for me, and that for many long years she had been doing so. I felt as if I could have jumped up and knelt beside her; but no, my proud heart would not let me, so I lay still, pretending to be asleep. But I didn't sleep that night. I soon changed my prayer; it was now, 'O God, save me; take away this terrible burden.' I didn't believe in Christ even yet. I thought I'd go right straight to the Father Himself. But the more I prayed I only became the more miserable; my burden grew heavier.

The next morning I did not wish to see my wife, so I said I was not well, and wouldn't wait for breakfast. I went to the office, and when the boy came I sent him home for a holiday. When the clerks came I told them they might go for the day. I closed the office doors: I wanted to be alone with God. I was almost frantic in my agony of heart. I cried to God to take away this load of sin. At last I fell on my knees, and cried, 'For Jesus Christ's sake take away this load of sin.' At length I went to my wife's pastor, who had been praying with her for my conversion for years, and the same minister who had prayed with my mother before she died. As I walked down the street the verse that my mother had taught me came into my mind, 'Whatsoever things you desire, when you pray, believe that you receive them, and you shall have them' [Mark 11]. Well, I thought, I have asked God, and here I am going to ask a man. I won't go.

I believe I am a Christian. I turned and went home. I met my wife in the hall as I entered. I caught her hand, and said, 'I am a Christian now.' She turned quite pale. She had been praying for twenty-one years for me, and yet she could not believe the answer had come. We went into our room, and knelt down by the very bedside where she had so often knelt to pray for her husband. There we erected our family altar, and for the first time our voices mingled in prayer. And I can only say that the last three months have been the happiest months ever I spent in my life." Since then that judge has lived a consistent Christian life; and all because he came to God, asking for guidance.

If there is one here today whose mind is filled with such infidel thoughts, go honestly to God, and He will teach you the right way through the dark wilderness of infidelity. He won't leave you in darkness or doubt. It is the devil's own work to lead men into such doubts. He knows well that once he gets them there he has them.

It is Satan's work to keep you in ignorance or doubt. It is God's work to teach you. The teacher is Christ. He has been appointed by God for this work.

God help us all to accept Him as our teacher.

Now we have seen Christ as our Savior, Redeemer, Deliverer, Leader, Light, and Teacher. But He is still more.

8. Christ is also Our SHEPHERD.

A very sweet thought it is to me, "The Lord is my Shepherd; I shall not want." There is not one here, except the very babes, who does not understand the work of a shepherd. He watches over his flock, protects them from danger, feeds them, leads them into the best pastures. In fact, the 23rd Psalm is just a statement of the duties of a good shepherd: "The Lord is my Shepherd; I shall not want," etc.

You want to be fed. Are you going to wander about seeking something to satisfy the cravings of your soul?

Then, I tell you, you never will find anything to satisfy the longings of your heart. The world cannot, and never could, satisfy a hungry soul. The Lord Jesus can—He is the true Shepherd. He is seeking to restore your soul, to lead you back to the paths of righteousness. Even to death will He lead you, and safely through its shadow guide you to a better land. Mother, father, will you claim Him as your Shepherd? Young man, young woman, will you have Him as your Shepherd? My little child, will you have Jesus as your Shepherd? He will lead safely and softly.

You can, all of you, if you will. For "God gave Him up freely for us all," that He might have us for His flock. He will lead us through life, down to the banks of the Jordan; He will lead us across the dark river into His kingdom. He is a tender, loving Shepherd.

I sometimes meet people in the anxious inquiry-room who are nourishing hard, bitter feelings against God, generally because they have been afflicted. A mother said to me the other day, "Ah, Mr. Moody, God has been unjust to me; He has come and taken away my child." Dear afflicted mothers, has God not removed your children to a pure and happy life? You may not understand it now, but you will by and by. He wants to lead you up there.

The Eastern Shepherd
A friend of mine, who had been in eastern lands, told me he saw a shepherd who wanted his flock to cross a river. He went into the water himself and called them; but no, they would not follow him into the water.

What did he do? Why, he girded up his loins and lifted a little lamb under each arm, and plunged right into the stream, and crossed it without even looking back.

Whenever he lifted the lambs, the old sheep looked up into his face and began to bleat for them; but when he plunged into the water the dams plunged after him, and then the whole flock followed. When they got to the other side he put down the lambs, and they were quickly joined by their mothers, and there was a happy meeting.

My friend says he noticed the pastures on the other side were much better and the fields greener, and on this account the shepherd was leading them across. Our great Palestine Shepherd does that. That child which He has taken from the earth is but removed to green pastures of Canaan, and the Shepherd means to draw your hearts after it, to teach you to "set your affections on things above." When He has taken your little Mary, Edith, or Julia, accept it as a call to look upward and beyond. You, mother, are you weeping bitter tears for your little one? Do not weep! Your child has gone to the place where there is neither weeping nor sorrow. Would you have it return? Surely never.

Christ is our Shepherd—faithful and loving. Though sickness, or trouble, or even death itself, should come to our house, and claim our dearest ones, still they are not lost, but only gone before. God help each one of us to have Him as our Shepherd.

If time permitted, I would take up the subject of Christ as our Justification, our Wisdom, our Righteousness, the Friend that sticks closer than a brother; but it would take a whole eternity to tell what Christ is to His people, and what He does for them.

I remember when I was preaching on this subject in Scotland, after I was done, I said to a man that "I was sorry I could not finish the subject for want of time." "Finish the subject," said the Scotchman, "why, that would require all eternity, and even then it would not be complete; it will be the occupation of heaven."

9. Christ as our BURDEN-BEARER.

Oh, I love to think of Him as the bearer of our burdens as well as our sin-bearer.

He carries our sins, although they are more numerous than the hairs of our heads. Great and terrible as these burdens are, God has laid them all on Jesus.

"O Christ, what burdens bowed Your head! Our load was laid on You." That aspect of His burden-bearing we have already looked at in His work as Savior and Redeemer. I wish now to take up the sweet thought, which has been a great comfort to me.

"Surely He has borne our griefs, and carried our sorrows." Glorious, is it not, to know we have such a Savior? Can you feel that He has lifted your burden off your shoulders on to His own shoulder? Then you will feel light in heart.

A Light Heart

On one occasion, after I had been talking this way, a woman came forward, and said, "Oh, Mr. Moody, it's all very well for you to talk like that, about a light heart. But you are a young man, and if you had a heavy burden like me you would talk differently. I could not talk in that way, my burden is too great." I replied, "But it's not too great for Jesus." "Oh," she said, "I cannot cast it on Him." "Why not? Surely it is not too great for Him. It is not that He is feeble. But it is because you will not leave it to Him. You're like many others. They will not leave it with Him. They go about hugging their burden, and yet crying out against it. What the Lord wants is, you to leave it with Him, to let Him carry it for you. Then you will have a light heart, sorrow will flee away, and there will be no more sighing. What is your burden, my friend, that you cannot leave with Christ?" She replied, "I have a son who is a wanderer on the face of the earth. None but God knows where he is." "Cannot Christ find him, and bring him back?" "I suppose He can." "Then go and tell Jesus, and ask Him to forgive you for doubting His power and willingness; you have no right to mistrust Him." She went away much comforted, and I believe she ultimately had her wandering boy restored to her!

A Mother's Prayer Answered
This circumstance reminds me of a faithful father and mother in our country, whose eldest son had gone to Chicago to a situation. A neighbor of theirs was in the city on some business, and he met the young man reeling along the streets drunk. He thought, "How am I to tell his parents?" When he returned to his village, he went and called out the father, and told him. It was a terrible blow to that father, but he said nothing to the mother till the little ones had all gone to rest. The servants had retired, and all was quiet in that little farm on the Western prairies. They drew up their chairs to the little drawing-room table, and then he told her the sad news. "Our boy has been seen drunk on the streets of Chicago—drunk." Ah, that mother was sorely hurt. They did not sleep much that night, but spent the hours in fervent prayers for their boy. About daybreak the mother felt an inward conviction that all would be well. She told the father "she had cast it on the Lord, had left her son with Jesus, and she felt He would save him."

One week from that time the young man left Chicago and took a journey of three hundred miles into the country; and when he reached his home, he walked in, and said, "Mother, I've come home to ask you to pray for me." Ah, her prayer had reached heaven; she had cast her burden on Jesus, and He had borne it for her. He took the burden, presented her prayer sprinkled with the atoning blood, and got it answered. In two days that young man returned to Chicago rejoicing in the Savior. What a wonderful thing it is to have Christ as our burden-bearer! How easy, how light do our cares become when cast upon Him!

Do you say Christ is nothing to you? If so, it is only because you won't have Him. He is to all who will accept Him a Savior from death, a Redeemer from the power of sin, a Deliverer from our enemies, a Leader through the wilderness. He is the way Himself, He is Light in the darkness, He is a Teacher to His people, He is the Shepherd of His flock, our Justification, Wisdom, Righteousness, Elder Brother, Burden-bearer.

He is in fact "Our all in all." Then come to Christ; oh, come today, The Father, Son, and Spirit say, The Bride repeats the call, For He will cleanse your guilty stains, His love will soothe your weary pains, For Christ is All in All.

Study Guide

Introduction

1. What, according to R.A. Torrey, were the seven things in Moody's life that enabled him to be used by God in such mighty ways?

2. Are these seven things characteristic of your life?

3. What is the secret power to which this book refers?

Biography

1. What was the effect of the Chicago fire of 1871 upon Moody's life and ministry?

2. What was Moody's attitude toward slavery and war?

3. What talented singer joined with Moody in the evangelistic ministry?

4. What term did Moody's children use to describe his faith?

5. With what illness was Moody afflicted in his later years?

Chapter 1—Power: Its Source

1. What, according to Moody, is the first work of the Holy Spirit?
2. Describe the personality of the Holy Spirit.
3. What is the role of divine love in the believer's life?
4. Which fruit of the Holy Spirit contains all the rest?
5. What happens in a person's life when he or she loses hope?
6. How can you overcome discouragement?
7. After imparting love and hope to us, what does the Holy Spirit give us?
8. Are you tapped into the source of power which Moody explains in this chapter?

Chapter 2—Power "In" and "Upon"

1. What are the three biblical dwelling places of the Holy Spirit?
2. Are you a temple of the Holy Ghost?
3. What is "the sword of the Spirit"?
4. What happens to us when we are filled with the Holy Spirit?
5. Why does the Holy Spirit come upon us?
6. What does Moody mean by "spiritual irrigation"?
7. Why do some people fail?
8. Do you desire power from on high? How can you receive it?

Chapter 3—Witnessing on Power

1. Jesus promised to send the Holy Spirit. What did He say the Holy Spirit would do?

2. What is the testimony of the Holy Spirit?

3. What did Moody say was the greatest miracle the world had ever seen?

4. Into what does the Holy Spirit guide us?

5. What do we learn from the Holy Spirit?

6. What does the Holy Spirit bring to our remembrance?

7. In what way does the Holy Spirit bring us comfort?

8. What is the role of the Holy Spirit in the life of a sinner?

9. List the eight different works of the Holy Spirit.

10. Are you seeking the guidance of the Holy Spirit for your life?

Chapter 4—Power in Operation

1. What, according to Moody, is God's standard for the believer's life?

2. What is the "badge" that Christ gave to His disciples?

3. What are the effects of love in a believer's life?

4. What comes after love?

5. What secures peace in our lives?

6. What is the difference between happiness and joy?

7. Have you entered into divine love, joy, and peace? How is it possible for you to do so?

Chapter 5—Power Hindered

1. What is the "unpardonable sin"?

2. In what ways can we grieve the Holy Spirit?

3. In what ways does the Church grieve the Holy Spirit?

4. What, according to Moody, is success?

5. In what ways might a person quench the Holy Spirit?

6. What are the emblems of the Holy Spirit?

7. Are you allowing the power of the Holy Spirit to flow from your life?

Gems From D.L. Moody

1. What happened when the Holy Spirit came upon the Son of Man?

2. What was the last teaching Jesus gave after He finished His work on Earth?

3. What enables a person to resist temptation?

4. How can you get out from under the power of evil and come under the power of God?

Sermon of D.L. Moody—"Christ Our All in All"

1. How do we experience the salvation Christ provides?

2. What does it mean to say that Christ is our Redeemer?

3. From what does the Lord deliver us?

4. How does the Lord Jesus Christ lead us and guide us?

5. Do you reflect the life of Christ in your life?

6. What does Jesus teach us?

7. As our Shepherd, what does Jesus do for us?

8. What must you do to let Jesus become your Burden-bearer?

9. Jesus is our Savior, Lord, Redeemer, Deliverer, Teacher, and Shepherd. What are some of His other roles in our lives?

10. Is Christ your all in all? What does this mean to you?

SUGGESTED READING

Albertson, Charles, C., *Gems of Truth and Beauty*, Rhodes and McClure, 1888.

Daniels, W. H., *D. L. Moody and His Work*, American Publishing Co., 1876.

Fitt, Arthur Percy, *The Life of D. L. Moody*, The Bible Institute Colportage Association, 1900.

Goodspeed, E. J., *The Wonderful Career of Moody and Sankey in Great Britain and America*, C. C. Wick & Co., 1876.

McClure, J. B., *Anecdotes and Illustrations of D. L. Moody*, Rhodes and McClure, 1881.

Moody, D. L., *Secret Power*, Fleming H. Revell, 1881.

Moody, D. L., *Brilliants*, H. M. Caldwell, 1894.

Moody, D. L., *Select Sermons*, Fleming H. Revell, 1880.

Torrey, R. A., *Why God Used D. L. Moody*, The Bible Institute Colportage Association, 1923.

INDEX

A

abolitionist 10
affection(s) 91
affections 141, 208
all in all 191, 211

B

Barnum, P. T. 22
Betsy Moody 3
Bible Institution's Colportage Association of Chicago 21
bitterness 94, 125, 170
blessing 81, 98, 113, 117, 135, 156, 178, 182, 187, 188, 189
bondage 158, 194
burden 189, 205, 209, 211

C

Calvary 137, 191, 198
captive 195
charity 92, 143, 145
child of God 85, 104, 142
children of light 201
Civil War 9
comfort 134, 152, 209
Comforter 84, 90, 123, 128, 132, 137
conviction 181, 210
conviction of sin 140
crown 91, 176

D

D. L. Moody and His Work x
darkness 109, 126, 128, 132, 155, 167, 188, 195, 196, 198, 201, 203, 206, 211
death 87, 109, 124, 126, 132, 137, 184, 207, 208, 211
delight 174

V

victory 106, 113

W

weakness 153, 188
Wisdom 208, 211
wisdom 109, 178, 202
work 85, 87, 91, 99, 102, 105, 107, 108, 113, 115, 116
  of Christ 124
  of God 81, 170, 181
  of the devil 206
  of the Spirit 84, 89, 94, 100, 107, 140, 168, 189
works 81, 125, 160
  of Satan 161
world, the 86, 90, 102, 104, 108, 113, 121, 125, 126, 128,
    132, 136, 138, 144, 149, 151, 152, 154, 159, 160, 161,
    162, 166, 169, 171, 172, 175, 176, 183, 184, 187, 189,
    192, 198, 199, 207

Y

YMCA 11, 13
Young Men's Mission Band 6

Pure Gold Classics

AN EXPANDING COLLECTION OF THE BEST-LOVED CHRISTIAN CLASSICS OF ALL TIME.

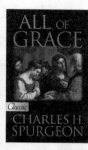
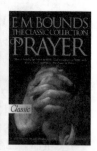

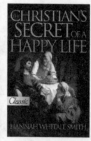

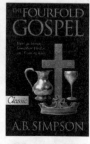
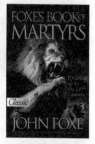

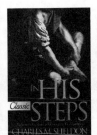

THE IMITATION OF CHRIST

Classic

THOMAS à KEMPIS

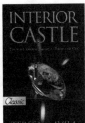

IN HIS STEPS

Classic

CHARLES M. SHELDON

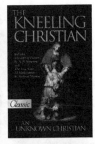

INTERIOR CASTLE

Classic

TERESA OF AVILA

THE KNEELING CHRISTIAN

Classic

AN UNKNOWN CHRISTIAN

MADAME JEANNE GUYON

Classic

EXPERIENCING UNION WITH GOD THROUGH INNER PRAYER & THE WAY AND RESULTS OF UNION WITH GOD

MORNING BY MORNING

Classic

CHARLES H. SPURGEON

THE OVERCOMING LIFE

Classic

D.L. MOODY

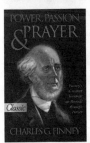

THE PILGRIM'S PROGRESS IN MODERN ENGLISH

Classic

JOHN BUNYAN

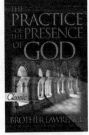

POWER, PASSION & PRAYER

Classic

CHARLES G. FINNEY

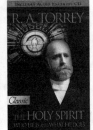

THE PRACTICE OF THE PRESENCE OF GOD

Classic

BROTHER LAWRENCE

R. A. TORREY

Classic

THE HOLY SPIRIT WHO HE IS AND WHAT HE DOES

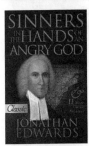

A SERIOUS CALL TO A DEVOUT & HOLY LIFE

Classic

WILLIAM LAW

SINNERS IN THE HANDS OF AN ANGRY GOD

Classic

JONATHAN EDWARDS

THE SOVEREIGNTY OF GOD

Classic

A.W. PINK

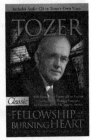

TABLE TALK

MARTIN LUTHER

Classic

TOZER

Classic

FELLOWSHIP OF THE BURNING HEART

TOZER ON THE HOLY SPIRIT

Classic

A.W. TOZER

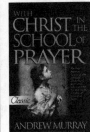

WALKING WITH GOD

Classic

THE ANDREW MURRAY TRILOGY OF SANCTIFICATION

WITH CHRIST IN THE SCHOOL OF PRAYER

Classic

ANDREW MURRAY

WILLIAM WILBERFORCE

Classic

GREATEST WORKS

Pure Gold Classics

CHRISTIAN CLASSICS

A classic is a work of enduring excellence; a Christian classic is a work of enduring excellence that is filled with divine wisdom, biblical revelation, and insights that are relevant to living a godly life. Such works are both spiritual and practical. Our Pure Gold Classics contain some of the finest examples of Christian writing that have ever been published, including the works of John Foxe, Charles Spurgeon, D.L. Moody, Martin Luther, John Calvin, Saint John of the Cross, E.M. Bounds, John Wesley, Andrew Murray, Hannah Whitall Smith, and many others.

The timeline on the following pages will help you to understand the context of the times in which these extraordinary books were written and the historical events that must have served to influence these great writers to create works that will always stand the test of time. Inspired by God, many of these authors did their work in difficult times and during periods of history that were not sympathetic to their message. Some even had to endure great persecution, misunderstanding, imprisonment, and martyrdom as a direct result of their writing.

The entries that are printed in green type will give you a good overview of Christian history from the birth of Jesus to modern times.

The entries in red pertain to writers of Christian classics from Saint Augustine, who wrote his *Confessions* and *City of God*, to Charles Sheldon, twentieth-century author of *In His Steps*.

Entries in black provide a clear perspective on the development of secular history from the early days of Buddhism (first century) through the Civil Rights Movement.

Finally, the blue entries highlight secular writers and artists, including Chaucer, Michelangelo, and others.

Our color timeline will provide you with a fresh perspective of history, both secular and Christian, and the classics, both secular and Christian. This perspective will help you to understand each author better and to see the world through his or her eyes.

-1770 George Whitefield, ...nist evangelist known ...owerful preaching ...revivals in England ...America. Friend of John ...y.

-1760 "The Great ...ening" in America. ...erous revivals result ...despread Church ...th.

...Handel's *Messiah* ...posed.

...-1763 Seven Years ...n Europe, Britain ...ats France.

...-1833 William ...erforce, British ...itionist and author of ...ctical View of ...stianity.

...-1783 American ...lutionary War.

... Olney Hymns ...ished, John Newton's ...zing Grace.

... French Revolution ...ns.

...2-1875 Charles ...ey, American ...gelist. Leads Second ...at Awakening in 1824.

...5-1898 George ...ller, English evangelist ...under of orphanages; ...or, *Answers to Prayer.*

...3-1855 Soren ...egaard, Danish ...osopher & theologian; ...or, *Fear and* ...bling.

...-1900 J.C. Ryle, ...or of *Practical Religion* ...Holiness.

1820-1915 "Fanny" Crosby, though blind, pens over 8,000 hymns.

1828-1917 Andrew Murray, author of *Humility, Abide in Christ, With Christ in the School of Prayer,* and *Absolute Surrender.*

1828 Noah Webster publishes a dictionary of the English Language.

1829 Salvation Army founded by William and Catherine Booth.

1832-1911 Hannah Whitall Smith, author of *The Christian's Secret to a Happy Life* and *God of All Comfort.*

1834-1892 Charles H. Spurgeon, author of *Morning by Morning* and *The Treasury of David.*

1835-1913 E.M. Bounds, author of *The Classic Collection on Prayer.*

1836-1895 A.J. Gordon, New England Spirit-filled pastor; author, *The Ministry of the Spirit.*

1837-1899 Dwight L. Moody, evangelist and founder of Moody Bible Institute in Chicago. Author of *Secret Power* and *The Way to God.*

1843-1919 A.B. Simpson, founder of Christian and Missionary Alliance; author of *The Fourfold Gospel.*

1844 Samuel Frank Morse invents the telegraph.

1847-1929 F.B. Meyer, English Baptist pastor & evangelist; author, *Secret of Guidance.*

1857-1858 Third Great Awakening in America; Prayer Meeting Revival.

1851-1897 Henry Drummond, author of *The Greatest Thing in the World … Love.*

1856-1928 R.A. Torrey, American evangelist, pastor and author.

1857-1946 Charles Sheldon, author of *In His Steps.*

1859 Theory of evolution; Charles Darwin's *Origin of Species.*

1861-1865 American Civil War.

1862-1935 Billy Sunday, American baseball player who became one of the most influential evangelists in the 20th century. *Collected Sermons.*

1867 Alexander Graham Bell invents the telephone.

1869-1948 Mahatma Gandhi makes his life's work India's peaceful independence from Britain.

1881-1936 J. Gresham Machen, "Old School" Presbyterian leader, writes *Christianity and Liberalism*; forms the new Orthodox Presbyterian Church in 1936.

1886-1952 A. W. Pink, evangelist & biblical scholar; author, *The Sovereignty of God.*

1897-1963 A.W. Tozer, author of *Fellowship of the Burning Heart.*

1898-1900 Boxer Rebellion in China deposes western influence, particularly Christian missionaries.

c. 1900-1930 *The Kneeling Christian* (Written by The Unknown Christian.)

1901 American Standard Version of Bible published.

1906 Azusa Street Revival, Los Angeles, instrumental in rise of modern Pentecostal Movement.

1906-1945 Dietrich Bonhoeffer spreads Christian faith to Germans in opposition to WWII Nazism.

1914-1918 World War I.

1917 Bolshevik Revolution in Russia.

1925 Scopes Monkey Trial pits Bible against theory of evolution.

1929 US Stock Market crashes, 12 years of Great Depression.

1939-1945 World War II. Holocaust in eastern Europe under Hitler.

1947 Dead Sea Scrolls found in caves in Judean desert.

1948 State of Israel reestablished.

1949 Communist revolution in China; religion suppressed.

1952 RSV Bible first published.

1960s Civil Rights movement in the United States.